Gnostic Gospels, including: Gospel Of Thomas, Nag Hammadi Library, Secret Gospel Of Mark, Gospel Of Philip, Gospel Of Mary, Gospel Of Judas, Unknown Berlin Gospel, Gospel Of Mani, Gospel Of Marcion, Gospel Of Truth, Gospel Of Basilides

Hephaestus Books

Contents

Articles

Gospel of Thomas   **1**

    Gospel of Thomas   1

Nag Hammadi library   **18**

    Nag Hammadi library   18

Secret Gospel of Mark   **25**

    Secret Gospel of Mark   25

Gospel of Philip   **35**

    Gospel of Philip   35

Gospel of Mary   **40**

    Gospel of Mary   40

Gospel of Judas   **46**

    Gospel of Judas   46

Unknown Berlin Gospel   **58**

    Unknown Berlin Gospel   58

Gospel of Mani   **60**

    Gospel of Mani   60

Gospel of Marcion   **61**

    Gospel of Marcion   61

Gospel of Truth 63

Gospel of Truth 63

Gnostic Gospels 68

Gnostic Gospels 68

Gospel of Basilides 72

Gospel of Basilides 72

Papyrus Oxyrhynchus L 3525 73

Papyrus Oxyrhynchus L 3525 73

Papyrus Rylands 463 75

Papyrus Rylands 463 75

The Secret Gospel of Mark and the Synoptic Problem 77

The Secret Gospel of Mark and the Synoptic Problem 77

References

Article Sources and Contributors 82

Image Sources, Licenses and Contributors 83

Gospel of Thomas

Gospel of Thomas

The Gospel According to Thomas, commonly shortened to the *Gospel of Thomas*, is a well preserved early Christian, non-canonical sayings-gospel discovered near Nag Hammadi, Egypt, in December 1945, in one of a group of books known as the Nag Hammadi library.

The Coptic language text, the second of seven contained in what modern-day scholars have designated as Codex II, is composed of 114 sayings attributed to Jesus. Almost half of these sayings more or less resemble those found in the Canonical Gospels, while the other sayings were previously unknown. Its place of origin may have been Syria, where Thomasine traditions were strong.

The introduction states: *These are the hidden words that the living Jesus spoke and Didymos Judas Thomas wrote them down.* Didymus (Greek) and Thomas (Aramaic) both mean "twin". Some scholars suspect that this reference to the Apostle Thomas is false, and that therefore the true author is unknown. The document probably originated within a school of early Christians, possibly proto-Gnostics Even the description of Thomas as a "gnostic" gospel is based upon little other than the fact that it was found along with gnostic texts at Nag Hammadi. The name of Thomas was also attached to the Book of Thomas the Contender, which was also in Nag Hammadi Codex II, and the Acts of Thomas.

The Gospel of Thomas is very different in tone and structure from other New Testament apocrypha and the four Canonical Gospels. Unlike the canonical Gospels, it is not a narrative account of the life of Jesus; instead, it consists of *logia* (sayings) attributed to Jesus, sometimes stand-alone, sometimes embedded in short dialogues or parables. The text contains a possible allusion to the death of Jesus in logion 65 (Parable of the Wicked Tenants, paralleled in the Synoptic Gospels), but doesn't mention crucifixion, resurrection, or final judgement; nor does it mention a messianic understanding of Jesus. The Early Church believed it to be a false gospel. Eusebius, for example, included it among a group of books that he believed to be not only spurious, but "the fictions of heretics" that should be thrown out as absurd and impious.

Finds and publication

The manuscript of the Coptic text, found in 1945 at Nag Hammadi, Egypt, is dated at around 340. It was first published in a photographic edition in 1956. This was followed three years later (1959) by the first English-language translation, with Coptic transcription. In 1977, James M. Robinson edited the first complete collection of English translations of the Nag Hammadi texts. The Gospel of Thomas has been translated and annotated worldwide in a wide variety of languages.

The original Coptic manuscript is now the property of the Coptic Museum in Cairo, Egypt, Department of Manuscripts.

Oxyrhynchus papyri fragments

After the Coptic version of the complete text was discovered in 1945 at Nag Hammadi, scholars soon realized that three different Greek text fragments previously found at Oxyrhynchus, also in Egypt, were part of the Gospel of Thomas. These three papyrus fragments of Thomas date to between 130 - 250 CE. Prior to the Nag Hammadi library discovery, the sayings of Jesus found in Oxyrhynchus were known simply as Logia Iesu. The corresponding Koine Greek fragments of the Gospel of Thomas, found in Oxyrhynchus are:

- P.Oxy. 1: fragments of logia 26 through 33, with the last two sentences of logion 77 in the Coptic version included at the end of logion 30 herein.
- P.Oxy. 654: fragments of the beginning through logion 7, logion 24 and logion 36 on the flip side of a papyrus containing surveying data.
- P.Oxy. 655: fragments of logia 36 through 39. 8 fragments designated *a* through *h*, whereof *f* and *h* have since been lost.

The wording of the Coptic sometimes differs markedly from the earlier Greek Oxyrhynchus texts, the extreme case being that the last portion of logion 30 in the Greek is found at the end of logion 77 in the Coptic. This fact, along with the quite different wording Hippolytus uses when apparently quoting it (see below), suggests that the Gospel of Thomas "may have circulated in more than one form and passed through several stages of redaction."

Although it is still generally assumed that the "Gospel of Thomas" was first composed in Greek, there is growing evidence that the Coptic Nag Hammadi text is a translation from Syriac. On comparing the Greek fragments from Oxyrhynchus with the fuller Coptic version, Nicholas Perrin argues that the differences can be attributed to the reliance of both on a common Syriac source.

Attestation

The earliest surviving written references to the *Gospel of Thomas* are found in the writings of Hippolytus of Rome (*c.* 222-235) and Origen of Alexandria (*c.* 233). Hippolytus wrote in his *Refutation of All Heresies* 5.7.20:

> "[The Naassenes] speak...of a nature which is both hidden and revealed at the same time and which they call the thought-for kingdom of heaven which is in a human being. They transmit a tradition concerning this in the Gospel entitled "According to Thomas," which states expressly, "The one who seeks me will find me in children of seven years and older, for there, hidden in the fourteenth aeon, I am revealed."

This appears to be a reference to saying 4 of Thomas, although the wording differs significantly.

Origen listed the "Gospel according to Thomas" as being among the heterodox apocryphal gospels known to him (*Hom. in Luc.* 1).

In the 4th and 5th centuries, various Church Fathers wrote that the Gospel of Thomas was highly valued by Mani. In the 4th century, Cyril of Jerusalem mentioned a "Gospel of Thomas" twice in his *Catechesis*: "The Manichæans also wrote a Gospel according to Thomas, which being tinctured with the fragrance of the evangelic title corrupts the souls of the simple sort." and "Let none read the Gospel according to Thomas: for it is the work not of one of the twelve Apostles, but of one of the three wicked disciples of Manes." The 5th century *Decretum Gelasianum* includes "A Gospel attributed to Thomas which the Manichaean use" in its list of heretical books.

Date of composition

Gnosticism
This article is part of a series on Gnosticism
Early Gnosticism
Syrian-Egyptic Gnosticism
Gnosticism in modern times
Philo
Simon Magus
Cerinthus
Valentinus
Basilides
Gnostic Gospels
Nag Hammadi library
Codex Tchacos
Askew Codex
Bruce Codex
Gnosticism and the New Testament

Gnosis
Neoplatonism and Gnosticism
Mandaeism
Manichaeism
Bosnian Church
Esoteric Christianity
Jnana
Gnosticism Portal

Richard Valantasis writes:

> Assigning a date to the Gospel of Thomas is very complex because it is difficult to know precisely to what a date is being assigned. Scholars have proposed a date as early as AD 60 or as late as AD 140, depending upon whether the Gospel of Thomas is identified with the original core of sayings, or with the author's published text, or with the Greek or Coptic texts, or with parallels in other literature.

Valantasis and other scholars argue that it is difficult to date Thomas because, as a collection of *logia* without a narrative framework, individual sayings could have been added to it gradually over time.

Robert E. Van Voorst states:

> Most interpreters place its writing in the second century, understanding that many of its oral traditions are much older.

Scholars generally fall into one of two main camps: an "early camp" favoring a date for the "core" of between the years 50 and 100, before or approximately contemporary with the composition of the canonical gospels and a "late camp" favoring a date in the 2nd century, after composition of the canonical gospels.

The early camp

Those who argue that Thomas dates from the first century use a variety of arguments.

Form of the gospel

Theissen and Merz argue the genre of a collection of sayings was one of the earliest forms in which material about Jesus was handed down. They assert that other collections of sayings, such as the Q document and the collection underlying Mark 4, were absorbed into larger narratives and no longer survive as independent documents, and that no later collections in this form survive. Meyer also asserts that the genre of a "sayings collection" is indicative of the first century, and that in particular the "use of parables without allegorical amplification" seems to antedate the canonical gospels. Maurice Casey has strongly questioned the argument from genre: the "logic of the argument requires that Q and the Gospel of Thomas be also dated at the same time as both the book of Proverbs and the *Sayings of Amen-em-Opet!*"

Independence from Synoptic Gospels

Stevan L. Davies argues that the apparent independence of the ordering of sayings in Thomas from that of their parallels in the synoptics shows that Thomas was most likely not reliant upon the canonical Gospels and probably predated them. A number of authors argue that when the logia in Thomas do have parallels in the synoptics the version in Thomas often seems closer to the source. Theissen and Merz give sayings 31 and 65 as examples of this. Koester agrees, citing especially the parables contained in sayings 8, 9, 57, 63, 64 and 65. In the few instances where the version in Thomas seems to be dependent on the Synoptics, Koester suggests, this may be due to the influence of the person who translated the text from Greek into Coptic.

Koester also argues that the absence of narrative materials (such as those found in the canonical gospels) in Thomas makes it unlikely that the gospel is "an eclectic excerpt from the gospels of the New Testament". He also cites the absence of the eschatological sayings characteristic of Q to show the independence of Thomas from that source.

Intertextuality with John's gospel

Another argument for an early date is what some scholars have suggested is an interplay between the Gospel of John and the *logia* of Thomas. Parallels between the two have been taken to suggest that Thomas' *logia* preceded John's work, and that the latter was making a point-by-point riposte to Thomas, either in real or mock conflict. This seeming dialectic has been pointed out by several New Testament scholars, notably Gregory J. Riley, April DeConick, and Elaine Pagels. Though differing in approach, they argue that several verses in the Gospel of John are best understood as responses to a Thomasine community and its beliefs. Pagels, for example, says that John's gospel makes two references to the inability of the world to recognize the divine light. In contrast, several of Thomas' sayings refer to the light born 'within'. John 1:9 ("...Light that lights every man born into the world") acknowledges Thomas' idea of the Light within. John also follows Thomas by personifying the Light as Jesus. John 14:16 ("I am the way, the truth, and the life...) and chapter 17, which emphasizes salvation via the *logos* of Christ, expands on Thomas' logion 1. Intertextuality and acknowledgment of Thomas' priority seems to be in play.

John's gospel is the only canonical one that gives Thomas the Apostle a dramatic role and spoken part, and Thomas is the only character therein described as having *apistos* (unbelief), in spite of the fact that virtually all the Johannine characters fail to live up to the author's standards of belief. With respect to the famous story of *Doubting Thomas*, it is suggested that John may have been denigrating or ridiculing a rival school of thought; however, this may be entirely tongue-in-cheek, as a sort of inside joke. In another apparent contrast, John's text matter-of-factly presents a bodily resurrection as if this is a *sine qua non* of the faith; in contrast, Thomas' insights about the spirit-and-body are more nuanced. For Thomas, resurrection seems more a cognitive event of spiritual attainment, one even involving a certain discipline or asceticism. Again, an apparently denigrating portrayal in the "Doubting Thomas" story may either be taken literally, or as a kind of mock "comeback" to Thomas' logia: not as an outright censuring of Thomas, but an improving gloss. After all, Thomas' thoughts about the spirit and body are really not so different from those which John has presented elsewhere. John portrays Thomas as physically touching the risen Jesus, inserting fingers and hands into his body, and ending with a shout. Pagels interprets this as signifying one-upmanship by John, who is forcing Thomas to acknowledge Jesus' bodily nature. She writes that "...he shows Thomas giving up his search for experiential truth – his 'unbelief' – to confess what John sees as the truth...". The point of these examples, as used by Riley and Pagels, is to support the argument that the text of Thomas must have existed and have gained a following at the time of the writing of John's Gospel, and that the importance of the Thomasine logia was great enough that John felt the necessity of weaving them into his own narrative.

As the scholarly debate continues on the issue of possible John-Thomas interplay, Christopher Skinner more recently responded in part to Riley, DeConick, and Pagels with *John and Thomas - Gospels in Conflict?* (Wipf and Stock, Princeton Theological Monograph Series 115, 2009).

Role of James

Albert Hogeterp argues that the Gospel's saying 12, which attributes leadership of the community to James the Just rather than to Peter, agrees with the description of the early Jerusalem church by Paul in Galatians 2:1-14 and may reflect a tradition predating AD 70. Meyer also lists "uncertainty about James the righteous, the brother of Jesus" as characteristic of a first century origin.

Depiction of Peter and Matthew

In saying 13, Peter and Matthew are depicted as unable to understand the true significance or identity of Jesus. Patterson argues that this can be interpreted as a criticism against the school of Christianity associated with the Gospel of Matthew, and that "[t]his sort of rivalry seems more at home in the first century than later", when all the apostles had become revered figures.

Parallel with Paul

According to Meyer, Thomas's saying 17: "I shall give you what no eye has seen, what no ear has heard and no hand has touched, and what has not come into the human heart", is strikingly similar to what Paul told the Corinthians he criticizes in Corinthians 1 2:9.

The late camp

The late camp dates *Thomas* some time after 100, generally in the mid-2nd century. They generally believe that although the text was composed around the mid-second century, it contains earlier sayings such as those originally found in the New Testament gospels of which *Thomas* was in some sense dependent in addition to inauthentic and possibly authentic independent sayings not found in any other extant text.

Dependence on the New Testament Gospels

A number of scholars have pointed out that the sayings in *Thomas* reflect conflations and harmonisations dependent on the canonical gospels. For example, saying 10 and 16 appear to contain a redacted harmonisation of Luke 12:4912:51-52and Matthew 10:34-35. In this case it has been suggested that the dependence is best explained by the author of *Thomas* making use of an earlier harmonised oral tradition based on Matthew and Luke.

Dependency on Luke's gospel

Another argument made for the late dating of Thomas is based upon the fact that Saying 5 in the original Greek (Papyrus Oxyrhynchus 654) seems to follow the vocabulary used in the gospel according to Luke (Luke 8:17), and not the vocabulary used in the gospel according to Mark (Mark 4:22). According to this argument - which presupposes firstly the rectitude of the Two-Source Hypothesis (widely held amongst current New Testament scholars), in which the author of Luke is seen as having used the pre-existing gospel according to Mark plus a lost Q document to compose his gospel - if the author of Thomas did, as Saying 5 suggests - refer to a pre-existing gospel according to Luke, rather than Mark's vocabulary, then the gospel of Thomas must have been composed subsequent to both Mark and Luke (the latter of which is dated to between 60AD - 90AD).

Another saying that employs similar vocabulary to that used in Luke rather than Mark is Saying 31 in the original Greek (Papyrus Oxyrhynchus 1), where Luke 4:23's term *dektos* (acceptable) 4:23 is employed rather than Mark 6:4's *atimos* (without honor). The word *dektos* (in all its cases and genders) is clearly typical of Luke, since it is only employed by him in the canonical gospels Luke 4:19; 4:24;Acts 10:35). Thus, the argument runs, the Greek Thomas has clearly been at least influenced by Luke's characteristic vocabulary.

According to John P. Meier, *c* 1990, scholars predominately conclude that Thomas depends on or harmonizes the Synoptics.

Syriac origin

A number of scholars argue that Thomas is dependent on Syriac writings, including unique versions of the canonical gospels. They contend that many sayings of the Gospel of Thomas are more similar to Syriac translations of the canonical gospels than their record in the original Greek. Craig A. Evans states that saying 54 in *Thomas*, which speaks of the poor and the kingdom of heaven, is more similar to the Syriac version of Matthew 5:3 than the Greek version of that passage or the parallel in Luke 6:20.

Klyne Snodgrass notes that saying 65-66 of *Thomas* containing the Parable of the Wicked Tenants appears to be dependent on the early harmonisation of Mark and Luke found in the old Syriac gospels. He concludes that, "*Thomas*, rather than representing the earliest form, has been shaped by this harmonizing tendency in Syria. If the *Gospel of Thomas* were the earliest, we would have to imagine that each of the evangelists or the traditions behind them expanded the parable in different directions and then that in the process of transmission the text was trimmed back to the form it has in the Syriac Gospels. It is much more likely that Thomas, which has a Syrian provenance, is dependent on the tradition of the canonical Gospels that has been abbreviated and harmonized by oral transmission."

Nicholas Perrin argues that *Thomas* is dependent on the *Diatessaron*, which was composed shortly after 172 by Tatian in Syria. Perrin explains the order of the sayings by attempting to demonstrate that almost all adjacent sayings are connected by Syriac catchwords, whereas in Coptic or Greek, catchwords have been found for only less than half of the pairs of adjacent sayings. Peter J. Williams analyzed Perrin's alleged Syriac catchwords and found them implausible. Robert Shedinger wrote that since Perrin attempts to reconstruct an Old Syriac version of Thomas without first establishing Thomas' reliance on the *Diatessaron*, Perrin's logic seems circular.

Lack of apocalyptic themes

The *Gospel of Thomas* and the New Testament Canon

The harsh and widespread reaction to Marcion's canon, the first New Testament canon known to have been created, may demonstrate that, by 140, it had become widely accepted that other texts formed parts of the records of the life and ministry of Jesus. Although arguments about some potential New Testament books, such as the *Shepherd of Hermas* and Book of Revelation, continued well into the 4th century, four canonical gospels, attributed to Matthew, Mark, Luke, and John, were accepted among orthodox Christians at least as early as the mid-2nd century. Tatian's widely used *Diatessaron*, compiled between 160 and 175, utilized the four gospels without any consideration of others. Irenaeus of Lyons wrote in the late 2nd century that *since there are four quarters of the earth ... it is fitting that the church should have four pillars ... the four Gospels* (*Against Heresies*, 3.11.8), and then shortly thereafter made the first known quotation from a fourth gospel—the canonical version of the Gospel of John. The late 2nd-century Muratorian fragment also recognizes only the three synoptic gospels and

John. Bible scholar Bruce Metzger wrote regarding the formation of the New Testament canon, "Although the fringes of the emerging canon remained unsettled for generations, a high degree of unanimity concerning the greater part of the New Testament was attained among the very diverse and scattered congregations of believers not only throughout the Mediterranean world, but also over an area extending from Britain to Mesopotamia."

It should be noted that information about the historical Jesus itself was not a singular criterion for inclusion into the New Testament Canon. Not all of the books that ended up in the New Testament contain information about the historical Jesus nor teachings from the historical Jesus, as evidenced by the Epistles and the book of Revelation.

The *Gospel of Thomas* may have been excluded from the canon of the New Testament because it was believed

- not to have been written close to the time of Jesus
- not to have been written by apostolic authority or was forged in Thomas' name
- not to have been used by multiple churches over a wide geographic range
- to be heretical or unorthodox
- not to have been useful or comprehensible
- to be secret - or for adepts - as the first sentence of the gospel declares.

The philosophy of the *Gospel of Thomas*

In the Thomas gospel, Jesus is presented as a spiritual guide whose words (when properly understood) bring eternal life (Saying 1). Readers of these sayings are advised to continue seeking until they find what will enable them to become rulers of their own lives (Saying 2) and thus to know themselves (Saying 3) and their legacy of being the children of "the living Father" (Saying 3). These goals are presented in the image of "entering the Kingdom" by the methodology of insight that goes beyond duality. (Saying 22). *The Gospel of Thomas* shows little or no concern for orthodox religious concepts and doctrines.

The Gospel of Thomas emphasizes direct and unmediated experience. In Thomas saying 108, Jesus says, "Whoever drinks from my mouth will become as I am; I myself shall become that person, and the hidden things will be revealed to him." Furthermore, salvation is personal and found through spiritual (psychological) introspection. In Thomas saying 70, Jesus says, "If you bring forth what is within you, what you have will save you. If you do not bring it forth, what you do not have within you will kill you." As such, this form of salvation is idiosyncratic and without literal explanation unless read from a psychological perspective related to Self vs. ego. In Thomas saying 3, Jesus says,

> ...the Kingdom of God is inside of you, and it is outside of you. When you come to know yourselves, then you will become known, and you will realize that it is you who are the sons of the living Father. But if you will not know yourselves, you dwell in poverty, and it is you who

are that poverty.

The teaching of salvation (i.e., entering the Kingdom of Heaven) that is found in *The Gospel of Thomas* is neither that of "works" nor of "grace" as the dichotomy is found in the canonical gospels, but what might be called a third way, that of insight. The overriding concern of *The Gospel of Thomas* is to find the light within in order to be a light unto the world. (See for example, Sayings 24, 26)

In contrast to the Gospel of John, where Jesus is likened to a (divine and beloved) Lord as in ruler, the Thomas gospel portrays Jesus as more the ubiquitous vehicle of spiritual inspiration and enlightenment, as in saying 77:

> I am the light that shines over all things. I am everything. From me all came forth, and to me all return. Split a piece of wood, and I am there. Lift a stone, and you will find me there.

In many other respects, the Thomas gospel offers terse yet familiar if not identical accounts of the sayings of Jesus as seen in the synoptic gospels.

Elaine Pagels, in her book *Beyond Belief*, argues that the Thomas gospel at first fell victim to the needs of the early Christian community for solidarity in the face of persecution, then to the will of the Emperor Constantine, who at the First Council of Nicaea in 325, wanted an end to the sectarian squabbling and a universal Christian creed. She goes on to point out that in spite of it being left out of the Catholic canon, being banned and sentenced to burn, many of the mystical elements have proven to reappear perennially in the works of mystics like Jacob Boehme, Teresa of Avila and Saint John of the Cross. She concludes that the Thomas gospel gives us a rare glimpse into the diversity of beliefs in the early Christian community, an alternative perspective to the Johannine gospel.

Importance and author

The *Gospel of Thomas* is regarded by some scholars as one of the most important texts in understanding early Christianity outside the New Testament. It is one of the earliest accounts of the teaching of Jesus outside of the canonical gospels, according to a few scholars, and so is considered a valuable text. It is further unique in that the gospel is no more than a collection of Jesus' sayings and parables, and contains no narrative account of his life, which is something that all four canonical gospels include.

No major Christian group accepts this gospel as canonical or authoritative. Nonetheless, it is an important work for scholars working on the Q document, which itself is thought to be a collection of sayings or teachings upon which Matthew and Luke are partly based. Although no copy of Q has ever been discovered, the fact that Thomas is similarly a 'sayings' Gospel is taken by some as indication that the early Christians did write collections of the sayings of Jesus, and thus they feel it renders the Q theory more credible.

By the time of its discovery, most scholars did not consider Apostle Thomas the author of this document and the author remained unknown. J. Menard produced a summary of the academic consensus in the mid-1970s which stated that the gospel was likely a very late text written by a Gnostic author, thus having very little relevance to the study of the early development of Christianity. Scholarly views of Gnosticism and the Gospel of Thomas have since become more nuanced and diverse.

In the 4th century Cyril of Jerusalem considered the author a disciple of Mani who was also called Thomas. Cyril stated:

> Mani had three disciples: Thomas, Baddas and Hermas. Let no one read the Gospel according to Thomas. For he is not one of the twelve apostles but one of the three wicked disciples of Mani.

Many scholars consider the *Gospel of Thomas* to be a gnostic text, since it was found in a library among others, it contains Gnostic themes, and perhaps presupposes a Gnostic worldview. Others reject this interpretation, because *Thomas* lacks the full-blown mythology of Gnosticism as described by Irenaeus of Lyons (ca. 185), and because Gnostics frequently appropriated and used a large "range of scripture from Genesis to the Psalms to Homer, from the Synoptics to John to the letters of Paul."

The Gospel of Thomas and the historical Jesus

Some modern scholars believe that the Gospel of Thomas was written independently of the canonical gospels, and therefore is a useful guide to historical Jesus research. Scholars may utilize one of a number of critical tools in biblical scholarship, the criterion of multiple attestation, to help build cases for historical reliability of the sayings of Jesus. By finding those sayings in the *Gospel of Thomas* that overlap with Q, Mark, Matthew, Luke, John, and Paul, scholars feel such sayings represent "multiple attestations" and therefore are more likely to come from a historical Jesus than sayings that are only singly attested.

Comparison of The *Gospel of Thomas* to the New Testament

The *Gospel of Thomas* does not refer to Jesus as "Christ", "Lord", or "Son of Man" as the New Testament does, but simply as "Jesus." The *Gospel of Thomas* also lacks any mention of Jesus' birth, baptism, miracles, travels, death, and resurrection. However, over half of the sayings in *Thomas* are similar to sayings and parables found in the canonical gospels.

The *Gospel of Thomas* does not list the canonical twelve apostles and it does not use either this expression or the terms "the twelve" or "the twelve disciples." It does mention James the Just, who is singled out ("No matter where you are you are to go to James the Just, for whose sake heaven and earth came into being"); Simon Peter; Matthew; Thomas, who is taken aside and receives three points of revelation; Mary; and Salome. Although here Mary (presumably Mary Magdalene) and Salome are mentioned among the disciples, the canonical gospels and *Acts* make a distinction between an inner group of twelve male disciples, with varying lists of names, and a larger group of disciples, among which there may well have been women. Despite the favorable mention of James the Just, generally considered a "pro-circumcision" Christian, the *Gospel of Thomas* also dismisses circumcision:

His disciples said to him, *"Is circumcision useful or not?"* He said to them, *"If it were useful, their father would produce children already circumcised from their mother. Rather, the true circumcision in spirit has become profitable in every respect."*

Compare Thomas 8 SV

8. *And Jesus said*, "The person is like a wise fisherman who cast his net into the sea and drew it up from the sea full of little fish. Among them the wise fisherman discovered a fine large fish. He threw all the little fish back into the sea, and easily chose the large fish. Anyone here with two good ears had better listen!"

with Matthew 13:47–50 NIV:

[47]"Once again, the kingdom of heaven is like a net that was let down into the lake and caught all kinds of fish. [48]When it was full, the fishermen pulled it up on the shore. Then they sat down and collected the good fish in baskets, but threw the bad away. [49]This is how it will be at the end of the age. The angels will come and separate the wicked from the righteous [50]and throw them into the fiery furnace, where there will be weeping and gnashing of teeth."

Another example is the parable of the lost sheep, which is paralleled by Matthew, Luke, John, and Thomas.

This is the parable of the lost sheep in Matthew 18:12–14 NIV

[12]"What do you think? If a man owns a hundred sheep, and one of them wanders away, will he not leave the ninety-nine on the hills and go to look for the one that wandered off? [13]And if he finds it, I tell you the truth, he is happier about that one sheep than about the ninety-nine that did not wander off. [14]In the same way your Father in heaven is not willing that any of these little ones should be lost."

This is the parable of the lost sheep in Luke 15: 3-7 NIV

[3]*Then Jesus told them this parable:* [4]"Suppose one of you has a hundred sheep and loses one of them. Does he not leave the ninety-nine in the open country and go after the lost sheep until he finds it? [5]And when he finds it, he joyfully puts it on his shoulders [6]and goes home. Then he calls his friends and neighbors together and says, 'Rejoice with me; I have found my lost sheep.' [7]I tell you that in the same way there will be more rejoicing in heaven over one sinner who repents than over ninety-nine righteous persons who do not need to repent."

This is the parable of the lost sheep in Thomas 107 SV

107. *Jesus said,* "The kingdom is like a shepherd who had a hundred sheep. One of them, the largest, went astray. He left the ninety-nine and looked for the one until he found it. After he had toiled, he said to the sheep, *I love you more than the ninety-nine."*

This is the lost sheep discourse in John 10: 1-18 NIV

[1]"I tell you the truth, the man who does not enter the sheep pen by the gate, but climbs in by some other way, is a thief and a robber. [2]The man who enters by the gate is the shepherd of his sheep. [3]The watchman opens the gate for him, and the sheep listen to his voice. He calls his own sheep by name and leads them out. [4]When he has brought out all his own, he goes on ahead of them, and his sheep follow him because they know his voice. [5]But they will never follow a stranger; in fact, they will run away from him because they do not recognize a stranger's voice." [6]Jesus used this figure of speech, but they did not understand what he was telling them.

[7]Therefore Jesus said again, "I tell you the truth, I am the gate for the sheep. [8]All who ever came before me were thieves and robbers, but the sheep did not listen to them. [9]I am the gate; whoever enters through me will be saved.[1] He will come in and go out, and find pasture. [10]The thief comes only to steal and kill and destroy; I have come that they may have life, and have it to the full. [11]"I am the good shepherd. The good shepherd lays down his life for the sheep. [12]The hired hand is not the shepherd who owns the sheep. So when he sees the wolf coming, he abandons the sheep and runs away. Then the wolf attacks the flock and scatters it. [13]The man runs away because he is a hired hand and cares nothing for the sheep.

[14]"I am the good shepherd; I know my sheep and my sheep know me — [15]just as the Father knows me and I know the Father — and I lay down my life for the sheep. [16]I have other sheep that are not of this sheep pen. I must bring them also. They too will listen to my voice, and there shall be one flock and one shepherd. [17]The reason my Father loves me is that I lay down my life — only to take it up again. [18]No one takes it from me, but I lay it down of my own accord. I have authority to lay it down and authority to take it up again. This command I received from my Father."

Other parallels include

- Matthew 10:16 parallels Thomas 39.
- Matthew 10:37 parallels Thomas 55 and 101
- Matthew 10:27b parallels Thomas 33a.
- Matthew 10:34–36 parallels Thomas 16.
- Matthew 10:26 parallels Thomas 5b.

Comparison Chart of the Major Gospels

The material in the Comparison Chart is from the *Gospel Parallels* by B. H. Throckmorton, *The five Gospels* by R. W. Funk, *The Gospel According to the Hebrews*, by E. B. Nicholson & *The Hebrew Gospel and the Development of the Synoptic Tradition* by J. R. Edwards.

Item	Matthew, Mark, Luke	John	Thomas	Gospel of the Hebrews
New Covenant	The central theme of the Gospels - Love God with all your heart and your neighbor as yourself	The central theme - Love is the New Commandment given by Jesus	Secret knowledge, love your friends	The central theme - Love one another
Forgiveness	Very important - particularly in Matthew and Luke	Assumed	Not mentioned	Very important - Forgiveness is a central theme and this gospel goes into the greatest detail
The Lord's Prayer	In Matthew & Luke but not Mark	Not mentioned	Not mentioned	Important - "mahar" or "tomorrow"
Love & the poor	Very Important - The rich young man	Assumed	Important	Very important - The rich young man
Jesus starts his ministry	Jesus meets John the Baptist and is baptized	Jesus meets John the Baptist	Only speaks of John the Baptist	Jesus meets John the Baptist and is baptized. This gospel goes into the greatest detail
Disciples-number	Twelve	Twelve	not mentioned	Twelve
Disciples-inner circle	Peter, Andrew, James & John	Peter, Andrew, James & the Beloved Disciple	Peter	Peter, Andrew, James, & John
Disciples-others	Philip, Bartholomew, Matthew, Thomas, James, Simon the Zealot, Jude Thaddaeus, & Judas	Philip, Nathanael, Matthew, Thomas, James, Simon the Zealot, Jude Thaddaeus & Judas	Matthew, Thomas, James the Just (Brother of Jesus)	Matthew, James the Just (Brother of Jesus), Simon the Zealot, Thaddaeus, Judas
Possible Authors	Unknown; Mark the Evangelist & Luke the Evangelist	The Beloved Disciple	Thomas	Matthew the Evangelist
Virgin birth account	In Matthew & Luke, but not Mark	Not mentioned	Not mentioned	Not mentioned
Jesus' baptism	Described	Not Mentioned	N/A	Described great detail

Preaching style	Brief one-liners; parables	Essay format, Midrash	Sayings, parables	Brief one-liners; parables
Storytelling	Parables	Figurative language & Metaphor	Gnostic, hidden, parables	Parables
Jesus' theology	1st Century liberal Judaism.	Critical of Jewish Authorities	Gnostic	1st Century Judaism
Miracles	Many miracles	Seven Signs	N/A	Fewer but more credible miracles
Duration of ministry	1 year	3 years (Multiple Passovers)	N/A	1 year
Location of ministry	Mainly Galilee	Mainly Judea, near Jerusalem	N/A	Mainly Galilee
Passover meal	Body & Blood = Bread and wine	Interrupts meal for foot washing	N/A	Hebrew Passover is celebrated but details are N/A Epiphanius
Burial shroud	A single piece of cloth	Multiple pieces of cloth	N/A	Given to the High Priest
Resurrection	Mary and the Women are the first to learn Jesus has arisen	John adds detailed account of Mary's experience of the Resurrection	Not Applicable as Gospel of Thomas is a collection of the "sayings" of Jesus, not the events of his life	In the Gospel of the Hebrews is the unique account of Jesus appearing to his brother, James the Just.

See also

- Five Trees
- Tree of Life
- *Stigmata*
- Common Sayings Source

References

- Davies, Stevan (1983). *The Gospel of Thomas and Christian Wisdom*. Seabury Press. ISBN081642456X
- DeConick, April. *Recovering the Original Gospel of Thomas: A History of the Gospel and Its Growth* (T&T Clark, 2005)
- Ehrman, Bart (2003). *Lost Scriptures: Books that Did Not Make it into the New Testament*. Oxford University Press, USA. ISBN 019-514182-2.

- Funk, Robert Walter and Roy W. Hoover, *The Five Gospels: What Did Jesus Really Say? the Search for the Authentic Words of Jesus*, Polebridge Press, 1993
- Guillaumont, Antoine Jean Baptiste, Henri-Charles Puech, G. Quispel, Walter Curt Till, and Yassah ʿAbd al-Masīh, eds. 1959. *Evangelium nach Thomas*. Leiden: E. J. Brill *Standard edition of the Coptic text*
- Koester, Helmut (1990). *Ancient Christian Gospels* [1]. Harrisburg, PA: Trinity Press International. ISBN 0334024501. Retrieved 2010-01-27.
- Layton, Bentley (1987). *The Gnostic Scriptures*. Doubleday. ISBN 0-385-47843-7.
- Layton, Bentley (1989). *Nag Hammadi Codex II*, 2 vols, E.J.Brill. The critical edition of the seven texts of Codex II, including the Gospel of Thomas. ISBN 90-04-08131-3
- Meyer, Marvin (2004). *The Gospel of Thomas: The Hidden Sayings of Jesus*. HarperCollins. ISBN 978-0-06-065581-5.
- Pagels, Elaine (2003). *Beyond Belief : The Secret Gospel of Thomas* (New York: Random House)
- Patterson, Stephen J; Robinson, James M.;Bethge, Hans-Gebhard (1998). *The Fifth Gospel: The Gospel of Thomas Comes of Age* [2]. Harrisburg, PA: Trinity Press International. ISBN 1563382490. Retrieved 2010-01-27.
- Perrin, Nicholas. *Thomas and Tatian: The Relationship between the Gospel of Thomas and the Diatessaron* (Academia Biblica 5; Atlanta : Society of Biblical Literature; Leiden : Brill, 2002).
- Perrin, Nicholas. *Thomas: The Other Gospel* (London, SPCK; Louisville, KY: Westminster John Knox: 2007).
- Robinson, James M. *et al.*, *The Nag Hammadi Library in English* (4th rev. ed.; Leiden; New York: E.J. Brill, 1996)
- Plisch, Uwe-Karsten (2007). *Das Thomasevangelium. Originaltext mit Kommentar*. Stuttgart: Deutsche Bibelgesellschaft. ISBN 3438051281.
- Snodgrass, Klyne R. "The Gospel of Thomas: A secondary Gospel," *Second Century* 7, 1989. pp. 19–30.
- Tuckett, Christopher M. "Thomas and the Synoptics," *Novum Testamentum* 30 (1988) 132-57, esp. p. 146.
- Valantasis, Richard (1997). *The Gospel of Thomas* [3]. London; New York: Routledge. ISBN 041511621X. Retrieved 2010-01-27.
- *The Facsimile Edition of the Nag Hammadi Codices: Codex II*. E.J.Brill (1974)

External links

- Gospel of Thomas Collection at The Gnosis Archive [4]
- Gospel of Thomas Homepage (Stevan Davies) [5]
- Gospel of Thomas at Early Christian Writings [6]
- Gospel of Thomas Collection [7] Commentary and Essays by Hugh McGregor Ross

Nag Hammadi library

Nag Hammadi library

The **Nag Hammadi library** is a collection of early Christian Gnostic texts discovered near the Upper Egyptian town of Nag Hammadi in 1945. That year, twelve leather-bound papyrus codices buried in a sealed jar were found by a local peasant named Mohammed Ali Samman. The writings in these codices comprised fifty-two mostly Gnostic treatises, but they also include three works belonging to the *Corpus Hermeticum* and a partial translation/alteration of Plato's *Republic*. In his "Introduction" to *The Nag Hammadi Library in English*, James Robinson suggests that

Codex IV is one of the texts discovered at Nag Hammadi

these codices may have belonged to a nearby Pachomian monastery, and were buried after Bishop Athanasius condemned the uncritical use of non-canonical books in his Festal Letter of 367 AD [1].

The Nag Hammadi codices are housed in the Coptic Museum in Cairo, Egypt. To read about their significance to modern scholarship into early Christianity, see the Gnosticism article.

Discovery at Nag Hammadi

Gnosticism

This article is part of a series on
Gnosticism

Early Gnosticism

Syrian-Egyptic Gnosticism

Gnosticism in modern times

Philo

Simon Magus

Cerinthus

Valentinus

Basilides

Gnostic Gospels

Nag Hammadi library

Codex Tchacos

Askew Codex

Bruce Codex

Gnosticism and the New Testament

Gnosis

Neoplatonism and Gnosticism

Mandaeism

Manichaeism

Bosnian Church

Esoteric Christianity

Jnana

Gnosticism Portal

The story of the discovery of the Nag Hammadi library in 1945 has been described as 'exciting as the contents of the find itself'. In December of that year, two Egyptian brothers found several papyri in a large earthenware vessel while digging for fertilizer around limestone caves near present-day Hamra Dom in Upper Egypt. The find was not initially reported by either of the brothers, who sought to make money from the manuscripts by selling them individually at intervals. It is also reported that the brothers' mother burned several of the manuscripts, worried, apparently, that the papers might have 'dangerous effects' (Markschies, *Gnosis*, 48). As a result, what came to be known as the Nag Hammadi library (owing to the proximity of the find to Nag Hammadi, the nearest major settlement) appeared only gradually, and its significance went unacknowledged until some time after its initial uncovering.

In 1946, the brothers became involved in a feud, and left the manuscripts with a Coptic priest, whose brother-in-law in October that year sold a codex to the Coptic Museum in Old Cairo (this tract is today numbered Codex III in the collection). The resident Coptologist and religious historian Jean Dorese, realizing the significance of the artifact, published the first reference to it in 1948. Over the years, most of the tracts were passed by the priest to a Cypriot antiques dealer in Cairo, thereafter being retained by the Department of Antiquities, for fear that they would be sold out of the country. After the revolution in 1956, these texts were handed to the Coptic Museum in Cairo, and declared national property. Pahor Labib, the director of the Coptic Museum at that time, was keen to keep these manuscripts in their country of origin.

Meanwhile, a single codex had been sold in Cairo to a Belgian antique dealer. After an attempt was made to sell the codex in both New York and Paris, it was acquired by the Carl Gustav Jung Institute in Zurich in 1951, through the mediation of Gilles Quispel. There it was intended as a birthday present to the famous psychologist; for this reason, this codex is typically known as the Jung Codex, being Codex I in the collection.

Jung's death in 1961 caused a quarrel over the ownership of the Jung Codex, with the result that the pages were not given to the Coptic Museum in Cairo until 1975, after a first edition of the text had been published. Thus the papyri were finally brought together in Cairo: of the 1945 find, eleven complete books and fragments of two others, 'amounting to well over 1000 written pages' are preserved there.

Translation

The first edition of a text found at Nag Hammadi was from the Jung Codex, a partial translation of which appeared in Cairo in 1956, and a single extensive facsimile edition was planned. Due to the difficult political circumstances in Egypt, individual tracts followed from the Cairo and Zurich collections only slowly.

This state of affairs changed only in 1966, with the holding of the Messina Congress in Italy. At this conference, intended to allow scholars to arrive at a group consensus concerning the definition of gnosticism, James M. Robinson, an expert on religion, assembled a group of editors and translators whose express task was to publish a bilingual edition of the Nag Hammadi codices in English, in collaboration with the Institute for Antiquity and Christianity [2] at the Claremont Graduate University in Claremont, California. Robinson had been elected secretary of the International Committee for the Nag Hammadi Codices, which had been formed in 1970 by UNESCO and the Egyptian Ministry of Culture; it was in this capacity that he oversaw the project. In the meantime, a facsimile edition in twelve volumes did appear between 1972 and 1977, with subsequent additions in 1979 and 1984 from publisher E.J. Brill in Leiden, called *The Facsimile Edition of the Nag Hammadi Codices*, making the whole find available for all interested parties to study in some form.

At the same time, in the German Democratic Republic a group of scholars - including Alexander Bohlig, Martin Krause and New Testament scholars Gesine Schenke, Hans-Martin Schenke and Hans-Gebhard Bethge - were preparing the first German translation of the find. The last three scholars prepared a complete scholarly translation under the auspices of the Berlin Humboldt University, which was published in 2001.

The James M. Robinson translation was first published in 1977, with the name *The Nag Hammadi Library in English*, in collaboration between E.J. Brill and Harper & Row. The single-volume publication, according to Robinson, 'marked the end of one stage of Nag Hammadi scholarship and the beginning of another' (from the Preface to the third revised edition). Paperback editions followed in 1981 and 1984, from E.J. Brill and Harper respectively. A third, completely revised edition was published in 1988. This marks the final stage in the gradual dispersal of gnostic texts into the wider public arena - the full complement of codices was finally available in unadulterated form to people around the world, in a variety of languages.

A further English edition was published in 1987, by Yale scholar Bentley Layton, called *The Gnostic Scriptures: A New Translation with Annotations* (Garden City: Doubleday & Co., 1987). The volume unified new translations from the Nag Hammadi Library with extracts from the heresiological writers, and other gnostic material. It remains, along with *The Nag Hammadi Library in English* one of the more accessible volumes translating the Nag Hammadi find, with extensive historical introductions to individual gnostic groups, notes on translation, annotations to the text and the organisation of tracts into clearly defined movements.

Complete list of codices found in Nag Hammadi

- Codex I (also known as *The Jung Foundation Codex*):
  - *The Prayer of the Apostle Paul*
  - *The Apocryphon of James* (also known as the Secret Book of James)
  - *The Gospel of Truth*
  - *The Treatise on the Resurrection*
  - *The Tripartite Tractate*
- Codex II:

- *The Apocryphon of John*
- *The Gospel of Thomas* a sayings gospel
- *The Gospel of Philip*
- *The Hypostasis of the Archons*
- *On the Origin of the World*
- *The Exegesis on the Soul*
- *The Book of Thomas the Contender*
- Codex III:
  - *The Apocryphon of John*
  - *The Gospel of the Egyptians*
  - *Eugnostos the Blessed*
  - *The Sophia of Jesus Christ*
  - *The Dialogue of the Saviour*
- Codex IV:
  - *The Apocryphon of John*
  - *The Gospel of the Egyptians*
- Codex V:
  - *Eugnostos the Blessed*
  - *The Apocalypse of Paul*
  - *The First Apocalypse of James*
  - *The Second Apocalypse of James*
  - *The Apocalypse of Adam*
- Codex VI:
  - *The Acts of Peter and the Twelve Apostles*
  - *The Thunder, Perfect Mind*
  - *Authoritative Teaching*
  - *The Concept of Our Great Power*
  - *Republic* by Plato - The original is not gnostic, but the Nag Hammadi library version is heavily modified with then-current gnostic concepts.
  - *The Discourse on the Eighth and Ninth* - a Hermetic treatise
  - *The Prayer of Thanksgiving* (with a hand-written note) - a Hermetic prayer
  - *Asclepius 21-29* - another Hermetic treatise
- Codex VII:
  - *The Paraphrase of Shem*
  - *The Second Treatise of the Great Seth*
  - *Gnostic Apocalypse of Peter*
  - *The Teachings of Silvanus*

- *The Three Steles of Seth*
- Codex VIII:
  - *Zostrianos*
  - *The Letter of Peter to Philip*
- Codex IX:
  - *Melchizedek*
  - *The Thought of Norea*
  - *The Testimony of truth*
- Codex X:
  - *Marsanes*
- Codex XI:
  - *The Interpretation of Knowledge*
  - *A Valentinian Exposition*, *On the Anointing*, *On Baptism* (A and B) and *On the Eucharist* (A and B)
  - *Allogenes*
  - *Hypsiphrone*
- Codex XII
  - *The Sentences of Sextus*
  - *The Gospel of Truth*
  - *Fragments*
- Codex XIII:
  - *Trimorphic Protennoia*
  - *On the Origin of the World*

The so-called "Codex XIII" is in fact not a codex, but rather the text of *Trimorphic Protennoia*, written on "... eight leaves removed from a thirteenth book in late antiquity and tucked inside the front cover of the sixth." (Robinson, NHLE, p. 10) Only a few lines from the beginning of *Origin of the World* are discernible on the bottom of the eighth leaf.

See also

- Apocalyptic literature
- Acts of the Apostles (genre)
- Agrapha
- Biblical archaeology
- Development of the New Testament canon
- Epistles
- Gnosticism

- Gospel of Mary Magdalene
- List of Gospels
- List of New Testament papyri
- New Testament apocrypha
- Pseudepigraphy
- Textual criticism

Further reading

- Layton, Bentley (1987). *The Gnostic Scriptures*. SCM Press. ISBN 0-334-02022-0. (526 pages)
- Markschies, Christoph (trans. John Bowden), (2000). *Gnosis: An Introduction*. T & T Clark. ISBN 0-567-08945-2. (145 pages)
- Pagels, Elaine (1979). *The Gnostic Gospels*. ISBN 0-679-72453-2. (182 pages)
- Robinson, James (1988). *The Nag Hammadi Library in English*. ISBN 0-06-066934-9. (549 pages)
- Robinson, James M., 1979 "The discovery of the Nag Hammadi codices," in *Biblical Archaeology* vol. 42, pp206–224.

External links

- The Gospel of Thomas [6]
- The Nag Hammadi THE GNOSTIC SOCIETY LIBRARY [3]
- The Nag Hammadi Library [4]
- How the manuscripts were found [5]

Secret Gospel of Mark

Secret Gospel of Mark

The **Secret Gospel of Mark** is a supposed non-canonical Christian gospel that is the subject of the Mar Saba letter, a previously unknown letter attributed to Clement of Alexandria that Morton Smith claimed to have found in Mar Saba monastery in 1958. The gospel is known exclusively from this letter, which contains two passages said to be quotations from it. The letter describes Secret Mark as an expanded version of the canonical Gospel of Mark with some episodes elucidated, written for an initiated elite.

Mark the Evangelist, by Bronzino, fresco 1525–28, in Barbadori Chapel, Florence

Smith claimed to have discovered the Mar Saba letter transcribed into the endpapers of a 17th-century printed edition of the works of Ignatius of Antioch. The finding caused a sensation, but was soon met with accusations of forgery. The situation was complicated when the original manuscript was transferred to another monastery and access was restricted (at this time, the manuscript is believed to be lost). Further research relied upon photographs and copies, including those made by Smith himself. Scholars have expressed a variety of opinions regarding the authenticity of the letter and the gospel described therein.

Content

In the Mar Saba letter, the Secret Gospel of Mark is described as a second "more spiritual" version of the Gospel of Mark composed by the evangelist himself. Its purpose was supposedly to encourage knowledge (*gnosis*) among more advanced Christians, and it was said to be in use in liturgies in Alexandria.

The letter includes two excerpts from the Secret Gospel. The first is to be inserted, Clement states, between what are verses 34 and 35 of Mark 10:

> And they come into Bethany. And a certain woman whose brother had died was there. And, coming, she prostrated herself before Jesus and says to him, 'Son of David, have mercy on me.' But the disciples rebuked her. And Jesus, being angered, went off with her into the garden where the tomb was, and straightway a great cry was heard from the tomb.

And going near Jesus rolled away the stone from the door of the tomb. And straightway, going in where the youth was, he stretched forth his hand and raised him, seizing his hand. But the youth, looking upon him, loved him and began to beseech him that he might be with him. And going out of the tomb they came into the house of the youth, for he was rich. And after six days Jesus told him what to do and in the evening the youth comes to him, wearing a linen cloth over his naked body. And he remained with him that night, for Jesus taught him the mystery of the kingdom of God. And thence, arising, he returned to the other side of the Jordan.

The second excerpt is very brief and is to be inserted, according to Clement, in Mark 10:46:

And the sister of the youth whom Jesus loved and his mother and Salome were there, and Jesus did not receive them.

While Clement endorses these two passages as authentic to the Secret Gospel of Mark, he rejects as a Carpocratian corruption the words "naked man with naked man".

Very shortly after the second excerpt, as Clement begins to explain the passages, the letter breaks off. Just before that, Clement says, "But the many other things about which you wrote both seem to be and are falsifications."

These two excerpts comprise the entirety of the Secret Gospel material. No separate text of the secret gospel is known to survive.

Stephen C. Carlson writes that the academic reception of *Secret Mark* is represented by Larry Hurtado as:

Furthermore, as a good many other scholars have concluded, it is inadvisable to rest too much on Secret Mark. The alleged letter of Clement that quotes it might be a forgery from more recent centuries. If the letter is genuine, the Secret Mark to which it refers may be at most an ancient but secondary edition of Mark produced in the second century by some group seeking to promote its own esoteric interests.

Lacunae and continuity

The two excerpts suggest resolutions to some puzzling passages in the canonical Mark.

The young man in the linen cloth

In Mark 14:51-52, a young man in a linen cloth is seized during Jesus' arrest, but he escapes at the cost of his clothing. This passage seems to have little to do with the rest of the narrative, and it has given cause to various interpretations. Often it is suggested that the young man is Mark himself. Some commentators believe that the boy was a stranger, who lived near the garden and, after being awakened, ran out, half-dressed, to see what all the noise was about (vv. 46-49). W. L. Lane thinks that Mark mentioned this episode in order to make it clear that "*all* (not only the disciples) fled, leaving

Jesus alone in the custody of the police." However these explanations are not entirely satisfactory.

The same Greek word *neaniskos* (*young man*) is used in both Secret Mark and at Mark 14:51. If we accept Helmut Koester's theory that the canonical Mark is a revision of Secret Mark, another explanation is possible: namely, that the ancient editor who deleted an earlier encounter of Jesus with such a young man in a cloth, then added this incident also involving a young man during Jesus' arrest.

There is another occurrence of *neaniskos* in Mark, this time as a youth dressed in white at the tomb of Jesus (Mark 16:5). For this particular passage, there are also parallel passages in both Matthew and Luke, but neither of the other Synoptic Gospels use the word *neaniskos*. (In Matthew 28:2 it is "an angel of the Lord" dressed in white that appears and, in Luke 24:4, there are *two* "men" (Greek: *andres*)). Thus, it is also possible that all three of these occurrences of *neaniskos* in Mark and in Secret Mark are somehow related. The proponents of Secret Mark as a forgery, on the other hand, suggest that Secret Mark was created based on Mark 14:51 and 16:5.

The lacuna in the trip to Jericho

The second excerpt fills in an apparent lacuna in Mark 10:46: "They came to Jericho. As he and his disciples and a large crowd were leaving Jericho, Bartimaeus son of Timaeus, a blind beggar, was sitting by the roadside."

The lack of any action in Jericho is interpreted by some as meaning that something has been lost from the text, and the second excerpt gives a brief encounter at this point.

Helmut Koester and Ron Cameron have argued that Secret Mark preceded the canonical Mark, and that the canonical Mark is in fact an abbreviation of Secret Mark.. This would explain the narrative discontinuity above. John Dominic Crossan has also been supportive of these views of Koester: "I consider that canonical Mark is a very deliberate revision of Secret Mark." More on the possible connection of Secret Mark to the Synoptic problem can be found in The Secret Gospel of Mark and the Synoptic Problem.

Secret Mark and the Gospel of John

The story of the resurrection of the young man by Jesus in Secret Mark bears clear similarities to the story of the raising of Lazarus in John's Gospel (John 11:1-44), and this was already noted by Morton Smith.

Smith tried to demonstrate that the resurrection story in Secret Mark does not contain any of the secondary traits found in the parallel story in John 11, and that the story in John 11 is more theologically developed. He concluded that the Secret Mark version of the story contains an older, independent, and more reliable witness to the oral tradition.

Helmut Koester agrees with Smith that the two stories are very close,

"That it is, in fact, the same story is evident in the emphasis upon the love between Jesus and the man who was raised by him (cf. John 11:3, 5, 35-36), expressed twice in the additions of Secret Mark. Both stories are also located in Bethany.

Further, Koester argues that the resurrection story in Secret Mark appears to be independent from that of John 11, and that the author of Secret Mark may have acquired it from some other source, possibly from the free tradition of stories about Jesus,

"But it is impossible that Secret Mark is dependent upon John 11. In its version of the story, there are no traces of the rather extensive Johannine redaction (proper names, motif of the delay of Jesus' travel, measurement of space and time, discourses of Jesus with his disciples and with Martha and Mary). As to its form, Secret Mark represents a stage of development of the story that corresponds to the source used by John. The author evidently still had access to the free tradition of stories about Jesus, or perhaps to some older written collection of miracle stories."

Issues of authenticity

The Secret Gospel is known only from the Mar Saba letter, which is itself only known from the copy discovered by Morton Smith. Therefore, logically, at least three important questions arise:

1. whether or not Mar Saba MS really contains a genuine letter of Clement
2. whether Clement's quotations from Secret Mark are accurate
3. whether these quotations reflect a genuine Marcan tradition

In 1982 Morton Smith summarized the state of the question as follows:

1. Attribution to Clement was accepted.
2. Clement's attribution of the excerpts to "Mark" was rejected.
3. The source of the excerpts was variously ascribed to a separate apocryphal gospel, a pastiche of canonical material, or an expansion of the canonical text using early material of unknown provenance.

Manuscript history

The authenticity of the Mar Saba letter itself has long been the subject of controversy. The manuscript and the book where it was found have disappeared; all that remains are black and white photographs made by Smith in 1958, and color photographs by a librarian ca 1976-1977. Early on, some scholars tended to discount Smith's claims because, as it was believed, the copy of the letter had been seen by no scholar other than Smith. Yet, in 1976, Guy G. Stroumsa and three other scholars relocated the document. The book was subsequently taken from Mar Saba to the library of the Greek Orthodox Patriarchate in Jerusalem in 1977, where the letter (i.e. the manuscript) was cut out of the book (on the back pages of which it was inscribed) as part of the library's scheme to house such material separately.

It was then photographed, by librarian Kallistos Dourvas.

The manuscript cannot now be relocated; the second photo series were only published in 2000. As of January 2009, the letter is only documented in the two sets of photographs. The ink and fiber were never subjected to examination.

Theories of Secret Mark as modern forgery

It is believed that the first scholar to suggest in print that Secret Mark was a modern forgery, possibly implicating Smith, was Quentin Quesnell, in his 1975 article.

The view of Secret Mark and the Mar Saba manuscript as modern forgeries was promoted after Morton Smith's death by Prof. Jacob Neusner, a specialist in ancient Judaism, who is believed to be the world's most published scholar in the humanities, with more than 900 books to his name. Neusner was Morton Smith's student and admirer but, later, in 1984, there was a very public falling out between them after Smith publicly denounced his former student's academic competence. Neusner subsequently described Secret Mark as the "forgery of the century". Yet Neusner never wrote any detailed analysis of Secret Mark, or an explanation of why he thought it was a forgery.

In 2001, scholar Philip Jenkins drew attention to a popular novel by James Hunter entitled *The Mystery of Mar Saba*, that first appeared in 1940. This novel presents some unusual parallels to the events associated with Mar Saba MS, that have unfolded in real life after 1958. Later, Robert M. Price also drew attention to this novel. In 2007, musicologist Peter Jeffery also published a book accusing Morton Smith of forgery, arguing that Smith wrote the Mar Saba document with the purpose of "creat(ing) the impression that Jesus practised homosexuality".

In 2005, writer Stephen Carlson published the book *The Gospel Hoax: Morton Smith's Invention of Secret Mark,* where he spells out his case that Morton Smith, himself, was both the author and the scribe of Mar Saba manuscript. When Carlson examined the photographs supplied by Smith, he claimed to observe a "forger's tremor." Thus, according to Carlson the letters had not actually been written at all, but drawn with shaky pen lines and with lifts of the pen in the middle of strokes. Carlson also claims that his comparisons with Morton Smith's typical rendering of Greek letters (such as in his own correspondence and notes) reveal that the unusual formation of the letters *theta* and *lambda* in the Mar Saba text matched Smith's own peculiar formation of those letters. Yet these claims by Carlson have been, in their own turn, challenged by subsequent scholarly research, especially by Scott G. Brown in numerous articles.

In 2010, another handwriting analysis of the Mar Saba MS was undertaken by a Greek graphologist Venetia Anastasopoulou at the behest of *Biblical Archaeology Review*. An internationally known Greek handwriting expert, she compared Mar Saba MS with known samples of Morton Smith's Greek handwriting, and concluded that it was most probably not written by Morton Smith.

Thus, a substantial number of respected academics and theologians have dismissed the allegations that Smith forged the letter.

Secret Mark as ancient or medieval forgery

Early on, there have been suggestions that, while Mar Saba manuscript may indeed be a genuine old manuscript, it could well contain an ancient or medieval forgery, based on canonical texts.

According to N. T. Wright most scholars who accept the text as genuine see in the Secret Gospel of Mark a considerably later gnostic adaptation of Mark in a gnostic direction. F. F. Bruce sees the story of the young man of Bethany clumsily based on the raising of Lazarus in the Gospel of John. Thus he sees the Secret Mark narrative as derivative, and denies that it could be either the source to the story of Lazarus, or an independent parallel.

Interpretation of *Secret Mark*

Baptismal significance

Until recently, the opinion has been very common that the raising of the young man, portrayed in Secret Mark, has primarily a baptismal significance, as a sort of a 'baptism of initiation.' This was the opinion that Smith himself originally proposed. Along these lines, the statement "Jesus taught him the mystery of the kingdom of God" was typically read as a reference to the rites of baptism.

But recently, there has been some debate about this matter. For example, Scott G. Brown (while defending the authenticity of Secret Mark) disagrees with Smith that the scene is a reference to baptism. Thus, he says, "[T]here is no mention of water or depiction of a baptism." He adds that "...the young man's linen sheet has baptismal connotations, but the text discourages every attempt to perceive Jesus literally baptizing him." S. Carlson seems to agree with Brown. The idea that Jesus practiced baptism is absent from the synoptic gospels, though it is introduced in the *Gospel of John.*

According to Brown, for Clement, "the mystery of the kingdom of God" meant primarily "advanced theological instruction." These matters have a bearing on the debates about the authenticity of Secret Mark, because Brown clearly implies that Smith, himself, did not quite understand his own discovery. Still, it may be pointed out that the placement of this incident within the chronology of the Gospel of Mark, i.e., just before the Passover celebrations, can imply some baptismal significance; the week before Easter/Passover is the preferred time for Christian baptism ceremonies.

Other interpretations

Scholar John Dart has proposed a complex theory of 'chiasms' (or 'chiasmus') running through the Gospel of Mark -- a type of literary devices he finds in the text. "He recovers a formal structure to original Mark containing five major chiastic spans framed by a prologue and a conclusion." According to Dart, his analysis supports the authenticity of Secret Mark.

In 2008, extensive correspondence between Smith and his teacher and lifelong friend Gershom Scholem was published, where they discuss Mar Saba MS over many years. The book's editor, Guy

Stroumsa, argues that Smith could not have forged the MS, because these letters "show him discussing the material with Scholem, over time, in ways that clearly reflect a process of discovery and reflection." Those letters can be interpreted differently. Smith wrote in 1948 that he was working on the early Fathers, "especially Clement of Alexandria" (p. 28). In 1955 Smith wrote that he was at work on a chapter "for a book on Mark" (p. 81). Later in 1955 Smith writes of "my book on Mark." (p. 85)

Nov/Dec 2009 issue of Biblical Archaeology Review (BAR 35:06) features a selection of articles dedicated to the Secret Gospel of Mark. It includes articles by Charles W. Hedrick, Hershel Shanks, and Helmut Koester. Generally, they are supportive of the authenticity of Mar Saba Ms.

The placement of the story within canonical Mark

If what is portrayed in Secret Mark is indeed a baptism, then the placement of this story within the canonical Mark is highly significant. What precedes the story is the third prediction of the Passion/Crucifixion (Mark 10:32-34). And what follows next is the story of the Sons of Zebedee (Mark 10:35-45), where baptism is mentioned explicitly. James and John ask Christ for positions of higher honor once Jesus is an earthly ruler. Jesus responds,

> "You do not know what you are asking. Are you able to drink the cup that I drink, or to be baptized with the baptism with which I am baptized?" (Mark 10:38)

Here baptism is clearly seen as a symbol of Jesus' coming crucifixion, and this is widely accepted by Christian commentators. This understanding of baptism seems to be based on the teachings of Paul, according to whom, those who "were baptized into Jesus Christ were baptized into his death" (Romans 6:3). Among the Synoptic gospels, only Mark mentions baptism in this passage; thus the interests of the author of Secret Mark parallel those of the author of Mark, which also parallel the teachings of Paul.

Smith's theories about the historical Jesus

In his later work, Morton Smith increasingly came to see the historical Jesus as practicing some type of magical rituals and hypnotism, thus explaining various healings of demoniacs in the gospels. Smith seems to have developed his "libertine" understanding of Jesus starting from about 1967. He carefully explored for any traces of a "libertine tradition" in early Christianity, and in the New Testament. Yet there's very little in the Mar Saba MS to give backing to any of this. This is illustrated by the fact that Smith devoted only 12 lines to Mar Saba MS in his book *Jesus the Magician*.

See also

- Mar Saba letter
- Morton Smith
- The Secret Gospel of Mark and the Synoptic Problem

References

- Smith, Morton. *The Secret Gospel: The Discovery and Interpretation of the Secret Gospel According to Mark*, London Victor Gollancz Ltd. 1974 ISBN 0-575-01801-1.
- Bethune, Brian. "Mark's Secret Gospel: What Does a Contested Text Say About Jesus, Gay Sex and Baptism?" *Maclean's.* May 12, 2005. [1]
- Bruce, F.F. "The 'Secret' Gospel of Mark." Ethel M. Wood Lecture. Delivered at the University of London. London, England, United Kingdom. February 11, 1974. [2]
- Brown, Scott G. *Mark's Other Gospel: Rethinking Morton's Smith Controversial Discovery* (ESCJ 15; Waterloo, Ont.: Wilfrid Laurier University Press, 2005) pp. xxiii + 332. ISBN 0-88920-491-6.
- Carlson, Stephen C. *Gospel Hoax: Morton Smith's Invention of Secret Mark.* Waco, Tex: Baylor University Press, 2005. ISBN 1-932792-48-1
- Crossan, John Dominic. *Birth of Christianity: Discovering what Happened in the Years Immediately After the Execution of Jesus.* New York: Continuum International Publishing Group, 1999. ISBN 0-567-08668-2
- Dart, John. *Decoding Mark*, Harrisburg, Pa.: Trinity Press International, 2003. Pp. ix + 213. Hardcover. $20.00. ISBN 1-56338-374-8.
- Ehrman, Bart. *Lost Christianities.* New York: Oxford University Press, 2005. ISBN 0195141832.
- Grafton, Anthony. "Gospel Secrets: The Biblical Controversies of Morton Smith." *The Nation.* January 26, 2009. [3]
- Harrington, Daniel J. "The Gospel According to Mark." In *The New Jerome Biblical Commentary.* 3rd ed. (reprint) Raymond E. Brown, Joseph A. Fitzmyer, and Roland E. Murphy, eds. New York: Prentice Hall, 1999. ISBN 0-13-859836-3
- Jeffery, Peter. *The Secret Gospel of Mark Unveiled: Imagined Rituals of Sex, Death, and Madness in a Biblical Forgery.* New Haven, Conn.: Yale University Press, 2007. ISBN 0-300-11760-4
- Lane, William L. *The Gospel of Mark, New International Commentary on the New Testament.* Rev. ed. Grand Rapids, Mich.: Eerdmans, 1974. ISBN 0-8028-2340-8
- Steinfels, Peter. "Was It a Hoax? Debate on a 'Secret Mark' Gospel Resumes." *New York Times.* March 31, 2007. [4]
- Stroumsa, Guy G., ed. *Morton Smith and Gershom Scholem, Correspondence 1945-1982.* Boston: Brill Academic Publishers, 2008. ISBN 90-04-16839-7
- Thiessen, Gerd and Merz, Annette. *The Historical Jesus: A Comprehensive Guide.* Minneapolis: Fortress Press, 1998. ISBN 0-8006-3122-6.

- Wright, N.T. *Jesus and the Victory of God: Christian Origins and the Question of God.* Vol. 2. Paperback ed. London: Society for Promoting Christian Knowledge Publishing, 1996. ISBN 0-281-04717-0

For further reading

- "Clement of Alexandria." In *New Catholic Encyclopedia.* Rev. exp. ed. Collegeveille, Minn.: Liturgical Press, 2004. [5] ISBN 0-8146-5962-4
- Eyer, Shawn. "The Strange Case of the Secret Gospel According to Mark: How Morton Smith's Discovery of a Lost Letter by Clement of Alexandria Scandalized Biblical Scholarship." *Alexandria: The Journal for the Western Cosmological Traditions.* 1995. [6]
- Fowler, Miles. "Identification of the Bethany Youth in the Secret Gospel of Mark With Other Figures Found in Mark and John." *Journal of Higher Criticism.* 5:1 (Spring 1998). [7]
- Grant, Robert M. *A Historical Introduction to the New Testament.* New York: Harper and Row, 1963.
- Charles W. Hedrick and Nikolaos Olympiou, *Secret Mark: New Photographs, New Witnesses.*, in "The Fourth R" 13:5 (2000): 3–11, 14–16. Contains color plates of the manuscript. (Available on-line.) [8]
- Jennings, Theodore W., Jr. *The Man Jesus Loved: Homoerotic Narratives from the New Testament.* Paperback ed. Cleveland, Ohio: Pilgrim Press, 2003. ISBN 0-8298-1535-X
- Metzger, Bruce. *A Textual Commentary on the Greek New Testament.* 2d rev. ed. New York: United Bible Societies, 2005. ISBN 1-59856-164-2
- Smith, Morton. *Clement of Alexandria and a Secret Gospel of Mark.* Cambridge, Mass.: Harvard University Press, 1973. ISBN 0-674-13490-7
- Smith, Morton. *The Secret Gospel: The Discovery and Interpretation of the Secret Gospel According to Mark.* 3rd ed. Middletown, Calif.: Dawn Horse Press, 2005. ISBN 1-57097-203-6
- Smith, Morton "Clement of Alexandria and Secret Mark: The Score at the End of the First Decade." *Harvard Theological Review.* October 1982.
- Smith, Morton. *Jesus, the Magician: Charlatan or Son of God?* Berkeley, Calif.: Ulysses Press, 1998. ISBN 1-56975-155-2
- Thackara, W.T.S. "Secret Gospels and Lost Christianities, Part I." *Sunrise.* December 2003/January 2004. [9]
- Thackara, W.T.S. "Secret Gospels and Lost Christianities, Part II." *Sunrise.* February/March 2004. [9]
- Thackara, W.T.S. "Secret Gospels and Lost Christianities, Part III." *Sunrise.* June/July 2004. [9]
- Thackara, W.T.S. "Secret Gospels and Lost Christianities, Part IV." *Sunrise.* August/September 2004. [9]

External links

- Translation by Morton Smith and Manuscript images [10]
- Kirby, Peter. "Secret Mark." Early Christian Writings Web site. [11]
- Price, Robert M. "Second Thoughts on the Secret Gospel." Robert M. Price Web site [12]
- Robinson, B.A. "The 'Secret Gospel of Mark': What happened to the copy of Clement's letter?" ReligiousTolerance.org [13] - Contains text of the Clementine letter, with several translations
- Did Morton Smith Forge 'Secret Mark'? A Handwriting Expert Weighs In [14] Biblical Archaeology Society

Gospel of Philip

Gospel of Philip

Gospel of Philip	
Date	ca. 180-350 AD
Attribution	None
Location	
Sources	
Manuscripts	Nag Hammadi library
Audience	
Theme	Christian Gnostic sacraments

The **Gospel of Philip** is one of the Gnostic Gospels, a text of New Testament apocrypha, dating back to around the third century but lost to modern researchers until an Egyptian peasant rediscovered it by accident, buried in a cave near Nag Hammadi, in 1945. Although this gospel may at first appear similar to the Gospel of Thomas, it is not a sayings gospel, but a collection of gnostic teachings and reflections, a "gnostic anthology", as Marvin Meyer has called it. Sacraments, in particular the sacrament of marriage, are a major theme. The text is perhaps most famous as a very early source for the idea that Jesus was married to Mary Magdalene. Though this is never explicitly stated in the document itself, she is described as Jesus' "lover" in some translations. Although the original text is missing from the papyrus scriptures discovered, some translations 'fill in' the gap, suggesting; "Jesus loved Mary Magdalene more than all the disciples and used to kiss her often on the mouth."

The text's title is modern; the only connection with Philip the Apostle is that he is the only apostle mentioned (at 73,8). The text makes no claim to be from Philip, though, similarly, the four New Testament gospels make no explicit claim to be written by Matthew, Mark, Luke or John. The Gospel of Philip was written between 150 AD and 300 AD, while Philip himself died 80 AD, making it extremely unlikely to be his writing. Most scholars hold a 3rd century date of composition.

History and context

A single manuscript of the *Gospel of Philip*, in Coptic, was found in the Nag Hammadi library, a cache of documents that was secreted in a jar and buried in the Egyptian desert at the end of the fourth century. The text was bound in the same codex that contained the better-known Gospel of Thomas.

Among the mix of aphorisms, parables, brief polemics, narrative dialogue, biblical exegesis (especially of *Genesis*), and dogmatic propositions, Wesley T. Isenberg, the editor and translator of the text, has enumerated seventeen sayings (*logia*) attributed to Jesus, nine of which are citations and interpretations of Jesus' words already found in the canonical gospels The new sayings, "identified by the formula introducing them ('he said', 'the Lord said', or 'the Saviour said') are brief and enigmatic and are best interpreted from a gnostic perspective," Isenberg has written in his *Introduction* to the text (see link).

Much of the Gospel of Philip is concerned with Gnostic views of the origin and nature of mankind and the sacraments of baptism, unction and marriage. The Gospel emphasizes the sacramental nature of the embrace between man and woman in the nuptial chamber, which is an archetype of spiritual unity, which entails the indissoluble nature of marriage Many of the sayings are identifiably gnostic, and often appear quite mysterious and enigmatic:

- *Blessed is he who is before he came into being. For he who is, has been and shall be.*
- *He who has knowledge of the truth is a free man, but the free man does not sin, for "He who sins is the slave of sin" [John 8:34]. Truth is the mother, knowledge the father.*
- *Echamoth is one thing and Echmoth, another. Echamoth is Wisdom simply, but Echmoth is the Wisdom of death, which is the one who knows death, which is called "the little Wisdom".*
- *Those who say they will die first and then rise are in error. If they do not first receive the resurrection while they live, when they die they will receive nothing.* (Compare with translation provided by the Nag Hammadi library: "Those who say that *the Lord* died first and then rose up are in error - for *He* rose up first and then died.)
- *Jesus came to crucify the world.*
- *Jesus took them all by stealth, for he did not appear as he was, but in the manner in which they would be able to see him. He appeared to them all. He appeared to the great as great. He appeared to the small as small. He appeared to the angels as an angel, and to men as a man.*
- *It is not possible for anyone to see anything of the things that actually exist unless he becomes like them... You saw the Spirit, you became spirit. You saw Christ, you became Christ. You saw the Father, you shall become Father. So in this place you see everything and do not see yourself, but in that place you do see yourself - and what you see you shall become.*
- *Adam came into being from two virgins, from the Spirit and from the virgin earth. Christ therefore, was born from a virgin to rectify the Fall which occurred in the beginning.*

One saying in particular appears to identify the levels of initiation in gnosticism, although what exactly the *bridal chamber* represented in gnostic thought is currently a matter of great debate:

> *The Lord did everything in a mystery, a baptism and a chrism and a eucharist and a redemption and a bridal chamber.*

Some Latter-Day Saints (Mormons) believe this "bridal chamber" to be a reference to a sacred and ancient rite to receive exaltation called "the new and everlasting covenant of marriage," or "eternal marriage."

Another interpretation of the Gospel of Philip finds Jesus as the central focus of the text. This view is supported by the Gnostic scholar, Marvin W. Meyer. Evidence for this belief can be found in the following selection of quotations from the gospel:

- *Those who receive the name of the father, the son, and holy spirit...[are] no longer a Christian, but [are] Christ.*
- *'My God, My God, why, lord, have you forsaken me?' [Jesus] spoke these words on the cross, for he had left that place.*
- *We are born again through the holy spirit, and we are conceived through Christ in baptism with two elements. We are anointed through the spirit, and when we are conceived, we were united.*
- *Jesus revealed himself at the Jordan River as the fullness of heaven's kingdom.*
- *As Jesus perfected the water of baptism, he poured out death. For this reason we go down into the water but not into death, that we may not be poured out into the spirit of the world.*

Thus, according to Meyer, it is clear that without Jesus, the rituals and mysteries mentioned in this gospel would have no context. Furthermore, this text seems to follow the beliefs of the Valentinian Christian sect, a group that worshipped the Gnostic Christ, and is often linked to what is sometimes thought to be Valentinius' own text, the Gospel of Truth.

The Gospel of Philip ends with its promise:

> *If anyone becomes a 'son of the bridechamber' he will receive the Light. If anyone does not receive it while he is in these places, he cannot receive it in the other place. He who receives any Light will not be seen, nor can he be held fast. No one will be able to trouble him in this way, whether he lives in the world or leaves the world. He has already received the Truth in images, and the World has become the Aeon. For the Aeon already exists for him as Pleroma, and he exists in this way. It is revealed to him alone, since it is not hidden in darkness and night but is hidden in a perfect Day and a holy Night.*

Mary Magdalene

The Gospel of Philip has been cited for the idea that Jesus married Mary Magdalene. Much of the Gospel of Philip is dedicated to a discussion of marriage as a sacred mystery, and two passages directly refer to Mary Magdalene and her close relationship with Jesus:

> There were three who always walked with the Lord: Mary, his mother, and her sister, and Magdalene, the one who was called his companion. His sister and his mother and his companion were each a Mary.

That passage is also interesting for its mention of Jesus's sister (Jesus's unnamed sisters are mentioned in the New Testament at Mark 6:3 [1]), although the text is confusing on that point: she appears to be described first as the sister of Jesus's mother Mary, then as the sister of Jesus, although this may be a translation problem. Mary Magdalene is called Jesus's companion, partner or consort, using the word *koinônos*, of Greek origin, and the word *hôtre*, of Egyptian origin. The other passage referring to Mary Magdalene is incomplete because of damage to the original manuscript. Several words are missing. The best guesses as to what they were are shown below in brackets. Most notably there is a hole in the manuscript after the phrase "and used to kiss her often on her...." But the passage appears to describe Jesus kissing Magdalene and using a parable to explain to the disciples why he loved her more than he loved them:

> And the companion of [the saviour was Mar]y Ma[gda]lene. [Christ loved] M[ary] more than [all] the disci[ples, and used to] kiss her [often] on her [mouth]. The rest of [the disciples were offended by it and expressed disapproval]. They said to him "Why do you love her more than all of us?" The Saviour answered and said to them, "Why do I not love you like her? When a blind man and one who sees are both together in darkness, they are no different from one another. When the light comes, then he who sees will see the light, and he who is blind will remain in darkness.

However, "mouth" is not necessarily the word after "kiss her... on her". It may have been another body part and simply shown respect.

Problems concerning the text

The *Gospel of Philip* is a text that reveals some connections with Early Christian writings of the Gnostic traditions. It is a series of *logia* or pithy aphoristic utterances, most of them apparently quotations and excerpts of lost writings, without any attempt at a narrative context. The main theme concerns the value of sacraments. Scholars debate whether the original language was Syriac or Greek. Wesley W. Isenberg, the text's translator, places the date "perhaps as late as the 2nd half of the 3rd century" and places its probable origin in Syria due to its references to Syriac words and eastern baptismal practices as well as its ascetic outlook. The on-line Early Christian Writings site gives it a date *ca* 180 − 250 [2] Second or third century dates is the range given in *The Ancient Mysteries: A*

Sourcebook, Marvin W.Meyer editor, 1987 p. 235.

Interpretation

The text has been interpreted by Isenberg (*The Nag Hammadi Library in English*, p. 141) as a Christian Gnostic sacramental catechesis. Bentley Layton identified it as a Valentinian anthology of excerpts, and Elaine Pagels and Martha Lee Turner have seen it as possessing a consistent and Valentinian theology. It is dismissed by Ian Wilson (*Jesus: The Evidence*, 2000 p.88) who argues that it "has no special claim to an early date, and seems to be merely a Mills and Boon-style fantasy of a type not uncommon among Christian apocryphal literature of the third and fourth centuries."

External links

- Wesley W. Isenberg, translator, *Gospel of Philip* [3]
- Early Christian writings [2]: *Gospel of Philip* brief introductions and e-texts
- Theology Website *Gospel of Philip* [4]: translation and complete introduction by Wesley W. Isenberg

References

- Leloup, *The Gospel Of Philip: Jesus, Mary Magdalene, And The Gnosis Of Sacred Union* 2004.
- Robinson, James M., *The Nag Hammadi Library* HarperCollins 1990. The standard translation.
- Smith, Andrew Phillip, 'The Gospel of Philip: Annotated and Explained,' Skylight Paths, 2005.
- Turner and McGuire, *Nag Hammadi Library After Fifty Years,*: Martha Lee Turner, "On the coherence of the *Gospel according to Philip*, pp 223 − 50 and Einar Thomasson, "How Valentinian is the Gospel of Philip?" pp 251 − 279.

Gospel of Mary

Gospel of Mary

Gospel of Mary	
Date	120–180 AD
Attribution	unknown
Location	
Sources	
Manuscripts	Berolinensis Gnosticus 8502,1 P. Oxyrhynchus 3525 P. Rylands 463
Audience	
Theme	The soul's ascent

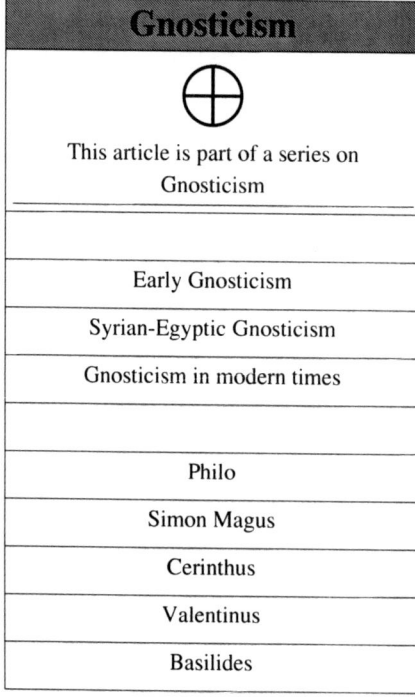

Gnosticism
This article is part of a series on Gnosticism
Early Gnosticism
Syrian-Egyptic Gnosticism
Gnosticism in modern times
Philo
Simon Magus
Cerinthus
Valentinus
Basilides

Gnostic Gospels
Nag Hammadi library
Codex Tchacos
Askew Codex
Bruce Codex
Gnosticism and the New Testament
Gnosis
Neoplatonism and Gnosticism
Mandaeism
Manichaeism
Bosnian Church
Esoteric Christianity
Jnana
Gnosticism Portal

The **Gospel of Mary** is an apocryphal book discovered in 1896 in a fifth-century papyrus codex. The codex Papyrus Berolinensis 8502 was purchased in Cairo by German scholar Karl Reinhardt.

Although the work is popularly known as the *Gospel of Mary*, it is not technically classed as a *gospel* by scholastic consensus. For example, Andrew Bernhard notes in his text-critical edition of non-canonical gospels that, "the term 'gospel' is used as a label for any written text that is primarily focused on recounting the teachings and/or activities of Jesus during His adult life."

History

Papyrus Berolinensis 8502, also known as the Akhmim Codex, also contains the *Apocryphon of John*, the *Sophia of Jesus Christ*, and a summary of the *Act of Peter*. All four works contained in the manuscript are written in Sahidic. Two other fragments of the *Gospel of Mary* have been discovered since, both written in Greek (Papyrus Oxyrhynchus L 3525 and Papyrus Rylands 463). P.Oxy. L 3525 "... was in fact found by Grenfell and Hunt some time between 1897 and 1906, but only published in 1983," by PJ Parsons.

- Image: P.Oxy. L 3525 [1] (© Copyright [2] the Egypt Exploration Society).

The two fragments were published respectively in 1938 and 1983, and the Coptic translation was published in 1955 by Walter Till.

Which Mary?

Scholars do not always agree which of the Marys in the New Testament is the central character of the *Gospel of Mary*. Arguments in favor of Mary Magdalene are based on her status as a known disciple of Jesus, the tradition of being the first witness of His resurrection, and her appearance in other early Christian writings. She is mentioned as accompanying Jesus on His journeys (Luke 8:2) and is listed in the Gospel of Matthew as being present at His crucifixion (27:56). In the Gospel of John, she is recorded as the first witness of Jesus' resurrection (John 20:14-16); (Mark 16:9 later manuscripts).

De Boer compares her role in other non-canonical texts, noting "in the Gospel of Mary it is Peter who is opposed to Mary's words, because she is a woman. Peter has the same role in the Gospel of Thomas and in Pistis Sophia. In Pistis Sophia the Mary concerned is identified as Mary Magdalene." The final scene in the Gospel of Mary may also provide evidence that Mary is indeed Mary Magdalene. Levi, in his defense of Mary and her teaching, tells Peter "Surely the Savior knows her very well. That is why he loved her more than us." In the Gospel of Philip, a similar statement is made about Mary Magdalene.

Aida Spencer, however, reviewing De Boer for the Journal of the Evangelical Theological Society, notes: "In summary, *Mary Magdalene* [the title of a study by De Boer] is an interesting, insightful, and intriguing historical study. However, the reader who is not capable of analyzing theories and who may be susceptible to the idea of an open canon may confuse a pleasant, respectable style with a potentially misleading theory."

King also argues in favor of naming Mary Magdalene as the central figure in the Gospel of Mary. She summarizes: "It was precisely the traditions of Mary as a woman, as an exemplary disciple, a witness to the ministry of Jesus, a visionary of the glorified Jesus, and someone traditionally in contest with Peter, that made her the only figure who could play all the roles required to convey the messages and meanings of the Gospel of Mary."

Contents

The most complete text of the Gospel of Mary is contained in Berolinensis 8502, but even so, it is missing six manuscript pages at the beginning of the document and four manuscript pages in the middle. As such, the narrative begins in the middle of a scene, leaving the setting and circumstances unclear. King believes, however, that references to the death of the Savior and the commissioning scene later in the narrative indicate the setting in the first section of the text is a post resurrection appearance of the Savior. As the narrative opens, the Savior is engaged in dialogue with his disciples, answering their questions on the nature of matter and the nature of sin. At the end of the discussion, the

Savior departs leaving the disciples distraught and anxious. According to the story, Mary speaks up with words of comfort and encouragement. Then Peter asks Mary to share with them any special teaching she received from the Savior, "Peter said to Mary, 'Sister, we know that the Savior loved you more than the rest of the women. Tell us the words of the Savior which you remember - which you know (but) we do not, nor have we heard them.'" Mary responds to Peter's request by recounting a conversation she had with the Savior about visions.

> "(Mary) said, 'I saw the Lord in a vision and I said to him, 'Lord, I saw you today in a vision.' He answered and said to me: "Blessed are you, that you did not waver at the sight of me. For where the mind is, there is the treasure.' I said to him, 'So now, Lord, does a person who sees a vision see it <through> the soul <or> through the spirit?'

In the conversation, the Savior teaches that the inner self is composed of soul, spirit, and mind, and visions are seen and understood in the mind. Then the text breaks off and the next four pages are missing. When the narrative resumes, Mary is no longer recalling her discussion with the Savior. She is instead recounting the revelation given to her in her vision. The revelation describes an ascent of a soul, which as it passes on its way to its final rest, engages in dialogue with four powers that try to stop it.

Her vision does not meet with universal approval:

> "But Andrew answered and said to the brethren, 'Say what you think concerning what she said. For I do not believe that the Savior said this. For certainly these teachings are of other ideas.'"

> "Peter also opposed her in regard to these matters and asked them about the Savior. 'Did he then speak secretly with a woman, in preference to us, and not openly? Are we to turn back and all listen to her? Did he prefer her to us?'"

However Levi defends Mary and quells Peter's attack on her. In the text, Peter appears to be offended by the discovery that Jesus selected Mary above the other disciples to interpret His teachings.

Interpretation

The Gospel of Mary is often interpreted as a Gnostic text. According to Pheme Perkins, on the basis of thirteen works, the Gospel follows a format similar to other known Gnostic dialogues which contain a revelation discourse framed by narrative elements. The dialogues are generally concerned with the idea of the Savior as reminder to human beings of their bond with God and true identity, as well as the realization of the believer that redemption consists of the return to God and liberty from matter after death. The Gospel of Mary contains two of these discourses (7.1-9.4 and 10.10-17.7) including addresses to New Testament characters (Peter, Mary, Andrew and Levi) and an explanation of sin as adultery (encouragement toward an ascetic lifestyle) which also suit a Gnostic interpretation. Scholars also note that the fifth-century Coptic version of the Gospel is part of the Berlin Codex along with the Apocryphon of John and the Sophia of Jesus Christ which are typically viewed as Gnostic texts. However, while many scholars take for granted the Gnostic character of the Gospel of Mary, the

Gnostic beliefs concerning creation theory and the Demiurge that would suggest an extreme dualism in the creation is not present in the portions currently retrieved (De Boer 2004).

De Boer (2004), however, suggests that the Gospel of Mary should not be read as a Gnostic specific text, but that it is to be "interpreted in the light of a broader Christian context". She argues that the Gospel stems from a monistic view of creation rather than the dualistic one central to Gnostic theology and also that the Gospel's views of both Nature and an opposite nature are more similar to Jewish, Christian, and Stoic beliefs. She suggests that the soul is not to be freed from Powers of Matter, but rather from the powers of the opposite nature. She also claims that the Gospel's main purpose is to encourage fearful disciples to go out and preach the gospel (De Boer 2004).

Karen King considers the work to provide

> an intriguing glimpse into a kind of Christianity lost for almost fifteen hundred years...[it] presents a radical interpretation of Jesus' teachings as a path to inner spiritual knowledge; it rejects His suffering and death as the path to eternal life; it exposes the erroneous view that Mary of Magdala was a prostitute for what it is—a piece of theological fiction; it presents the most straightforward and convincing argument in any early Christian writing for the legitimacy of women's leadership; it offers a sharp critique of illegitimate power and a utopian vision of spiritual perfection; it challenges our rather romantic views about the harmony and unanimity of the first Christians; and it asks us to rethink the basis for church authority."

King concludes that "both the content and the text's structure lead the reader inward toward the identity, power and freedom of the true self, the soul set free from the Powers of Matter and the fear of death." "The Gospel of Mary is about inter-Christian controversies, the reliability of the disciples' witness, the validity of teachings given to the disciples through post-resurrection revelation and vision, and the leadership of women" (De Boer 2004).

King also sees evidence for tensions within second-century Christianity, reflected in "the confrontation of Mary with Peter, [which is] a scenario also found in *The Gospel of Thomas*, *Pistis Sophia*, and the *Coptic Gospel of the Egyptians*. Peter and Andrew represent orthodox positions which deny the validity of esoteric revelation and reject the authority of women to teach."

Manuscripts

- Papyrus Oxyrhynchus L 3525
- Papyrus Rylands 463

References

- "Gospel of Mary". Nag Hammadi Studies Volume XI. Douglas M. Parrott, ed. Leiden: E.J. Brill, 1979.
- Meyer, Marvin. The Gospels of mary. San Francisco: Harper, 2004.
- King, Karen L., *The Gospel of Mary of Magdala: Jesus and the First Woman Apostle*. Santa Rosa: Polebridge Press, 2003.
- De Boer, Esther A., *The Gospel of Mary Listening to the Beloved Disciple*. London: Continuum, 2006 (2005).
- De Boer, Esther A., *The Gospel of Mary: Beyond a Gnostic and a Biblican Mary Magdalene*. London: Continuum, 2004.

External links

Details of manuscripts:

- Early Christian Writings: [3] *Gospel of Mary*

Translations:

- Gospel of Mary [4] Text from the Papyrus Berolinensis
- *Gospel of Mary* [5]: (English), syncretic text, incorporating Coptic and earlier Greek versions; further web links

Discussion:

- Eric Thurman, 'The Gospel of Mary: Alternative Authority in Early Christian History' [6], *American Bible Society website*.
- EI Sanchez, Gospel of Mary [7] (conservative response)

Related sites:

- Secrets of Mary Magdalene Website [8]
- Gospel of Mary Magdalene [9] from the Official Site for *The Lost Tomb of Jesus* [10]

Other:

- Gospel of Mary [11]
- Gnostic Judas [12] The Gospel of Mary Magdalene

Gospel of Judas

Gospel of Judas

Gospel of Judas	
Date	before 180, mentioned by Irenaeus
Attribution	no attribution
Location	El Minya, Egypt near Beni Mazar,
Sources	no academic consensus
Manuscripts	Codex Tchacos, references in early Christian writings
Audience	Cainites / Sethians - Gnostic sects
Theme	Judas as the chosen disciple, Gnostic cosmology

The **Gospel of Judas** is a Gnostic gospel purported to document conversations between the apostle Judas Iscariot and Jesus Christ. The document is not claimed to have been written by Judas himself, but rather by Gnostic followers of Jesus. It exists in an early fourth-century Coptic text, though it has been proposed, but not proven, that the text is a translation of an earlier Greek version. The Gospel of Judas is probably from no earlier than the second century, since it contains theology that is not represented before the second half of the second century, and since its introduction and epilogue assume the reader is familiar with the canonical Gospels. The oldest Coptic document has been carbon dated to AD 280, plus or minus 50 years.

First page of the Gospel of Judas
(Page 33 of Codex Tchacos)

According to the canonical Gospels of the New Testament (Matthew, Mark, Luke, and John), Judas identified Jesus to Jerusalem's Temple authorities, who handed Jesus over to Pontius Pilate, representative of the occupying Roman Empire, for crucifixion. The Gospel of Judas, on the other hand, portrays Judas in a very different perspective than do the Gospels of the New Testament, according to a preliminary translation made in early 2006 by the

National Geographic Society: the Gospel of Judas appears to interpret Judas's act not as betrayal, but rather as an act of obedience to the instructions of Jesus. This assumption is taken on the basis that Jesus required a second agent to set in motion a course of events which he had planned. In that sense Judas acted as a catalyst. The action of Judas, then, was a pivotal point which interconnected a series of simultaneous pre-orchestrated events.

This portrayal seems to conform to a notion current in some forms of Gnosticism, that the human form is a spiritual prison, that Judas thus served Christ by helping to release Christ's soul from its physical constraints, and that two kinds of human beings exist: the men furnished with the immortal soul which is "from the eternal realms" and "will abide there always" ("the strong and holy generation...with no ruler over it", to whom Judas belongs), and the other ones, the majority of mankind, who are mortal and therefore unable to reach the salvation. The Gospel of Judas does not claim that the other disciples knew gnostic teachings. On the contrary, it asserts that they had not learned the true Gospel, which Jesus taught only to Judas Iscariot, the sole follower belonging to the "holy generation" among the disciples.

Background

Gnosticism
This article is part of a series on Gnosticism
Early Gnosticism
Syrian-Egyptic Gnosticism
Gnosticism in modern times
Philo
Simon Magus
Cerinthus
Valentinus
Basilides
Gnostic Gospels
Nag Hammadi library

Codex Tchacos
Askew Codex
Bruce Codex
Gnosticism and the New Testament
Gnosis
Neoplatonism and Gnosticism
Mandaeism
Manichaeism
Bosnian Church
Esoteric Christianity
Jnana
Gnosticism Portal

The codex Tchacos, a leather-bound Coptic papyrus may have been discovered during the 1970s, near Beni Masah in Egypt. This has been translated and appears to be a text from the late 2nd [1] century A.D. describing the story of Jesus's death from the viewpoint of Judas. The conclusion of the text refers (in Coptic) to the text as "the Gospel of Judas" (*Euangelion Ioudas*).

According to a 2006 translation of the manuscript of the text, it is apparently a Gnostic account of an arrangement between Jesus and Judas, who in this telling are Gnostic enlightened beings, with Jesus asking Judas to turn him in to the Romans to help Jesus finish his appointed task from God.

During the second and third centuries AD, various Christian sects composed texts which are loosely labeled New Testament Apocrypha; these texts like those in the New Testament, are usually but not always "pseudeponymous", i.e. falsely attributed to a notable figure, such as an apostle, of an earlier era.

The text is extant in only one manuscript, a fourth-century Coptic manuscript known as the Codex Tchacos, which surfaced in the 1970s, after about sixteen centuries in the desert of Egypt. The existing manuscript was radiocarbon dated "between the third and fourth century", according to Timothy Jull, a carbon-dating expert at the University of Arizona's physics centre. Only sections of papyrus containing no text were carbon-dated, because carbon dating is physically destructive.

Today the manuscript is in over a thousand pieces, due to poor handling and storage, with many sections missing. In some cases, there are only scattered words; in others, many lines. According to Rodolphe Kasser, the codex originally contained 31 pages, with writing on front and back; when it came to the market in 1999, only 13 pages, with writing on front and back, remained. It is speculated that individual pages had been removed and sold.

It has been speculated, on the basis of textual analysis concerning features of dialect and Greek loan words, that the current Coptic fourth century text may be a translation from an older Greek manuscript dating, at the earliest, to approximately AD 130–180. Cited in support is the reference to a "Gospel of Judas" by the early Christian writer Irenaeus of Lyons, who, in arguing against Gnosticism, called the text a "fictitious history" (*Refutation of Gnosticism*, bk. 1 ch. 31). However, it is uncertain whether this text mentioned by Irenaeus is in fact the same text as the Coptic "Gospel of Judas" of the extant fourth century text, and there remains no solid evidence for an early Greek version.

A. J. Levine, who was on the team of scholars responsible for unveiling the work, emphatically stated that the Gospel of Judas contains no new historical information concerning Jesus or Judas. However, the text is helpful in reconstructing the history of Gnosticism, especially in Coptic-speaking areas.

Content

Ancient controversy

Irenaeus mentions a *Gospel of Judas* in his anti-Gnostic work *Adversus Haereses* (Against Heresies), written in about 180. He writes there are some who

> declare that Cain derived his being from the Power above, and acknowledge that Esau, Korah, the Sodomites, and all such persons, are related to themselves. . .They declare that Judas the traitor was thoroughly acquainted with these things, and that he alone, knowing the truth as no others did, accomplished the mystery of the betrayal; by him all things, both earthly and heavenly, were thus thrown into confusion. They produce a fictional history of this kind, which they style the *Gospel of Judas.*

This is in reference to the Cainites, an alleged sect of Gnosticism that especially worshipped Cain as a hero. Irenaeus alleged that the Cainites, like a large number of Gnostic groups, were semi-maltheists believing that the god of the Old Testament — Yahweh — was evil, and a quite different and much lesser being than the deity that had created the universe, and who was responsible for sending Jesus. Such Gnostic groups worshipped as heroes all the Biblical figures who had sought to discover knowledge or challenge Yahweh's authority, while demonizing those who would have been seen as heroes in a more orthodox interpretation.

The Gospel of Judas belongs to a school of Gnosticism called Sethianism, a group who looked to Adam's son Seth as their spiritual ancestor. As in other Sethian documents, Jesus is equated with Seth: "The first is Seth, who is called Christ" although this is in part of an emanationist mythology describing both positive and negative aeons.

For metaphysical reasons, the Sethian Gnostics authors of this text maintained that Judas acted as he did in order that mankind might be redeemed by the death of Jesus' mortal body. For this reason, they regarded Judas as worthy of gratitude and veneration. The Gospel of Judas does not describe any events after the arrest of Jesus.

By contrast, the canonical Gospel of John, unlike the synoptic gospels, asserts that Jesus said to Judas, as the latter left the Last Supper to set in motion the betrayal process, "Do quickly what you have to do." (trans. *The New English Bible*) John 13:27. Interpretations include: this was a direct command to Judas to do what he did; Jesus was speaking to Satan rather than to Judas (thus "Satan entered into Judas"); or Jesus knew what Judas was secretly plotting.

Some two centuries after Irenaeus' complaint, Epiphanius of Salamis, bishop of Cyprus, criticized the Gospel of Judas for treating as commendable the person whom he saw as the betrayer of Jesus, and as one who "performed a good work for our salvation." (*Haeres.*, xxxviii).

The Gospel of Judas itself attacking other beliefs

According to the Gospel, Judas was the only one of Jesus' followers fully to understand the Gnostic teachings: "Knowing that Judas was reflecting upon something that was exalted, Jesus said to him: Step away from the others and I shall tell you the mysteries of the Kingdom. It is possible for you to reach it, but you will grieve a great deal. For someone else will replace you, in order that the twelve disciples may again come to completion with their God."

The Gospel of Judas goes even further, showing Jesus in various instances criticizing the other disciples for their ignorance and their followers of immorality.

When they tell Jesus about a vision, he points out its true meaning as follows: "Those you have seen receiving the offerings at the altar — that is who you are. That is the God you serve, and you are those twelve men you have seen. The cattle you saw brought for sacrifice are the many people you lead astray before that altar. (. . .) will stand and make use of my name in this way, and generations of the pious will remain loyal to Him."

Modern rediscovery

The initial translation of the *Gospel of Judas* was widely publicized but simply confirmed the account that was written in Irenaeus and known Gnostic beliefs, leading some scholars to simply summarize the discovery as nothing new.

However, it is argued that a closer reading of the existent text, as presented in October 2006, shows that Judas may have been set up to actually betray Jesus out of wrath and anger:

> Truly [I] say to you, Judas, [those who] offer sacrifices to Saklas, the great fool, [... *exemplify* ...] everything that is evil. But you will exceed all of them. For you will sacrifice the man that clothes me. Already your horn has been raised, your wrath has been kindled, your star has shone brightly, and your heart has [*been hardened...*]

The initial translators might have been misled by Irenaeus' summary, which although an exciting idea was not necessarily accurate. Their theory is now in dispute.

According to Elaine Pagels, Bible translators have mistranslated the Greek word for "handing over" to "betrayal".

Like many Gnostic works, the *Gospel of Judas* claims to be a secret account, specifically "the secret account of the revelation that Jesus spoke in conversation with Judas Iscariot."

Over the ages many philosophers have contemplated the idea that Judas was required to have carried out his actions in order for Jesus to have died on the cross and hence fulfill theological obligations. The *Gospel of Judas*, however, asserts clearly that Judas' action was in obedience to a direct command of Jesus himself.

The *Gospel of Judas* states that Jesus told Judas "You shall be cursed for generations" and then added, "You will come to rule over them" and "You will exceed all of them, for you will sacrifice the man that clothes me."

Unlike the four canonical gospels, which employ narrative accounts of the last year of life of Jesus (in the case of John, three years) and of his birth (in the case of Luke and Matthew), the Judas gospel takes the form of dialogues between Jesus and Judas, and Jesus and the twelve disciples, without being embedded in any narrative or worked into any overt philosophical or rhetorical context. Such "dialogue gospels" were popular during the early decades of Christianity, and indeed the four canonical gospels are the only surviving gospels in narrative form. The New Testament apocrypha contains several examples of the dialogue form, an example being the Gospel of Mary Magdalene.

Like the canonical gospels, the Gospel of Judas portrays the scribes as approaching Judas with the intention of arresting him, and Judas receiving money from them after handing Jesus over to them. But unlike Judas in the canonical gospels, who is portrayed as a villain, and excoriated by Jesus ("Alas for that man by whom the Son of Man is betrayed. It would be better for that man if he had never been born," trans. *The New English Bible*) Mark 14:21; Matthew 26:24, the Judas gospel portrays Judas as a divinely appointed instrument of a grand and predetermined purpose. "In the last days they will curse your ascent to the holy (generation)."

Elsewhere in the manuscript, Jesus favours Judas above other disciples by saying, "Step away from the others and I shall tell you the mysteries of the kingdom," and "Look, you have been told everything. Lift up your eyes and look at the cloud and the light within it and the stars surrounding it. The star that leads the way is your star."

In the New Testament, Judas is said to have died by hanging himself (Matthew 27:3-10), or by bursting open after a fall (Acts 1:16-19). The *Gospel of Judas* does not specify the fate of Judas, although in the gospel, Judas tells Jesus he has had a vision where he is stoned to death by the eleven remaining apostles.

Rediscovery

Origins

The content of the gospel had been unknown until a Coptic *Gospel of Judas* turned up on the antiquities "grey market," in Geneva in May 1983, when it was found among a mixed group of Greek and Coptic manuscripts offered to Stephen Emmel, a Yale Ph.D. candidate commissioned by Southern Methodist University to inspect the manuscripts. How this manuscript, Codex Tchacos, was found, maybe in the late 1970s, has not been clearly documented. However, it is believed that a now-deceased Egyptian "treasure-hunter" or prospector discovered the codex near El Minya, Egypt, in the neighbourhood of the village Beni Masar, and sold it to one Hanna, a dealer in antiquities resident in Cairo.

"The Kiss of Judas" is a traditional depiction of Judas by Giotto di Bondone, c. 1306. Fresco in the Scrovegni Chapel, Padua.

In the 1970s, the manuscript and most of the dealer's other artifacts were stolen by a Greek trader named Nikolas Koutoulakis, and smuggled into Geneva. Hanna, along with Swiss antiquity traders, paid Koutoulakis a sum rumoured to be between $3 million to $10 million, recovered the manuscript and introduced it to experts who recognized its significance.

Sale and study

During the following two decades the manuscript was quietly offered to prospective buyers, but no major library or Egypt felt ready to purchase a manuscript that had such questionable provenance. In 2003 Michel van Rijn started to publish material about these dubious negotiations, and eventually the 62-page leather-bound codex was purchased by the Maecenas Foundation in Basel, a private foundation directed by lawyer Mario Jean Roberty. The previous owners now claimed that it had been uncovered at Muhafazat al Minya in Egypt during the 1950s or 1960s, and that its significance had not been appreciated until recently. It is worth noting that various other locations had been alleged during previous negotiations.

The existence of the text was made public by Rodolphe Kasser at a conference of Coptic specialists in Paris, July 2004. In a statement issued March 30, 2005, a spokesman for the Maecenas Foundation announced plans for edited translations into English, French, German, and Polish once the fragile papyrus has undergone conservation by a team of specialists in Coptic history to be led by a former professor at the University of Geneva, Rodolphe Kasser, and that their work would be published in about a year. A. J. Tim Jull, director of the National Science Foundation Arizona AMS laboratory, and Gregory Hodgins, assistant research scientist, announced that a radiocarbon dating procedure had dated five samples from the papyrus manuscript from 220 to 340 in January 2005 at the University of Arizona. This puts the Coptic manuscript in the third or fourth centuries, a century earlier than had originally been thought from analysis of the script. In January 2006, Gene A. Ware of the Papyrological Imaging Lab of Brigham Young University conducted a multi-spectral imaging process on the texts in Switzerland, and confirmed their authenticity.

Over the decades, the manuscript had been handled with less than sympathetic care: some single pages may be loose on the antiquities market (one half page turned up in Feb. 2006, in New York City); the text is now in over a thousand pieces and fragments, and is believed to be less than three-quarters complete. "After concluding the research, everything will be returned to Egypt. The work belongs there and they will be conserved in the best way," Roberty has stated.

In April 2006, an Ohio bankruptcy lawyer claimed to possess several small, brown bits of papyrus from the Gospel of Judas, but he refuses to have the fragments authenticated and his claim is being viewed with skepticism by experts.

Responses and reactions

Scholarly debates

Professor Kasser revealed a few details about the text in 2004, the Dutch paper *Het Parool* reported. Its language is the same Sahidic dialect of Coptic in which Coptic texts of the Nag Hammadi Library are written. The codex has four parts: the *Letter of Peter to Philip*, already known from the Nag Hammadi Library; the *First Apocalypse of James*, also known from the Nag Hammadi Library; the first few pages of a work related to, but not the same as, the Nag Hammadi work *Allogenes*; and the *Gospel of Judas*. Up to a third of the codex is currently illegible.

A scientific paper was to be published in 2005, but was delayed. The completion of the restoration and translation was announced by the National Geographic Society at a news conference in Washington, D.C. on April 6, 2006, and the manuscript itself was unveiled then at the National Geographic Society headquarters, accompanied by a television special entitled *The Gospel of Judas* on April 9, 2006, which was aired on the National Geographic Channel.

One scholar on the National Geographic project believes the document shows that Judas was "fooled" into believing he was helping Jesus.

The National Geographic Society responded that 'Virtually all issues April D. DeConick raises about translation choices are addressed in footnotes in both the popular and critical editions'.

André Gagné, Professor at Concordia University in Montreal also questioned how the experts of the National Geographic Society (NGS) understood the role of Judas Iscariot in the Gospel of Judas. His argument rests on the translation of the Greco-Coptic term *apophasis* as *denial*. According to Gagné, the opening lines of the Judas Gospel should *not* be translated as "the secret word of **declaration** by which Jesus spoke in conversation with Judas Iscariot" but rather as "the secret word of the *denial* by which Jesus spoke in conversation with Judas Iscariot" (Gospel of Judas 33:1). Gagné's conclusion is that this gospel is the story of the *denial* of true salvation for Judas.

Religious responses

In his 2006 Easter address, Rowan Williams, the Archbishop of Canterbury, strongly denied the historical credibility of the gospel, saying

> This is a demonstrably late text which simply parallels a large number of quite well-known works from the more eccentric fringes of the early century Church.

He went on to suggest that the book's publicity derives from an insatiable desire for conspiracy theories:

> We are instantly fascinated by the suggestion of conspiracies and cover-ups; this has become so much the stuff of our imagination these days that it is only natural, it seems, to expect it when we turn to ancient texts, especially biblical texts. We treat them as if they were unconvincing press releases from some official source, whose intention is to conceal the real story; and that real story waits for the intrepid investigator to uncover it and share it with the waiting world. Anything that looks like the official version is automatically suspect.

Later the same year, Biblical scholar Louis Painchaud argued that the text suggests Judas was actually possessed by a demon.

The uniqueness of the codex

The president of the Maecenas Foundation, Mario Roberty, suggested the possibility that the Maecenas Foundation had acquired not the only *extant* copy of the Gospel, but rather the only *known* copy. Roberty went on to make the suggestion that the Vatican probably had another copy locked away, saying:

> In those days the Church decided for political reasons to include the Gospels of Matthew, Mark, Luke, and John in the Bible. The other gospels were banned. It is highly logical that the Catholic Church would have kept a copy of the forbidden gospels. Sadly, the Vatican does not want to clarify further. Their policy has been the same for years — 'No further comment.'

Roberty provided no evidence to suggest that the Vatican does, in fact, possess any additional copy. While the contents of one part of the Vatican library have been catalogued and have long been available to researchers and scholars, the remainder of the library is, however, without a public catalogue, and though researchers may view any work within, they must first name the text they require, a serious problem for those who do not know what is contained by the library. The Pope responded on April 13, 2006-

> The Vatican, by word of Pope Benedict XVI, grants the recently surfaced Judas' Gospel no credit with regards to its apocryphal claims that Judas betrayed Jesus in compliance with the latter's own requests. According to the Pope, Judas freely chose to betray Jesus: "an open rejection of God's love". Judas, according to Pope Benedict XVI "viewed Jesus in terms of power and success: his only real interests lay in his power and success, there was no love involved. He was a greedy man: money was more important than communing with Jesus; money came before God and his love". According to the Pope it was due to these traits that led Judas to "turn liar, two-faced, indifferent to the truth", "losing any sense of God", "turning hard, incapable of converting, of being the prodigal son, hence throwing away a spent existence".

Spokespersons say the Vatican does not wish to suppress the Gospel of Judas; rather, according to Monsignor Walter Brandmüller, president of the Vatican's Committee for Historical Science, "We welcome the [manuscript] like we welcome the critical study of any text of ancient literature". Even more explicitly, Father Thomas D. Williams, Dean of Theology at the *Regina Apostolorum* university in Rome, when asked:

> Is it true that the Catholic Church has tried to cover up this text [Gospel of Judas] and other apocryphal texts?

answered as follows:

> These are myths circulated by Dan Brown (who wrote/recorded them purely as part of a fictional novel) and numerous conspiracy theorists. You can go to any Catholic bookstore and pick up a copy of the Gnostic gospels. Christians may not believe them to be true, but there is no attempt to hide them.

In AD 367, the bishop of Alexandria did urge Christians to "cleanse the church from every defilement" and to reject "the hidden books." It is highly possible that, in response to letters such as this one, some Christians destroyed or buried non-canonical gospels.

See also

- Lost work
- *The Passover Plot* (1965), a book by the Biblical scholar Hugh J. Schonfield
- *Tres versiones de Judas* (1944), a short story by Jorge Luis Borges (from the collection *Ficciones*) in which a fictional Swedish theologian claims that Judas is the real savior of mankind
- *The Last Temptation of Christ* (1951), a novel by Nikos Kazantzakis (and film by Martin Scorsese) that depicts Judas in a similar vein to the Gospel of Judas
- *Beelzebub's Tales to His Grandson* (1950), by G. I. Gurdjieff, presents Judas in accordance with his depiction in the Gospel of Judas

- *The Way of Cross and Dragon* (1979), a short story by George R. R. Martin that includes a fictional Gospel of Judas
- *The Judas Testament* (1994), a novel by Daniel Easterman about the discovery of an autobiography of the historical Jesus
- *The Gospel According to Judas* (2007), a novel by Jeffrey Archer and Frank Moloney that presents the events of the New Testament through the eyes of Judas Iscariot
- Jedi Mind Tricks mention the Gospel of Judas in their song Heavy Metal Kings.
- *A Time for Judas* (1983), a novel by Morley Callaghan where plot is extremely similar to the content revealed in the Gospel of Judas

References

- *The Gospel of Judas* [2]. Trans. and Eds. Rodolphe Kasser, Marvin Meyer, and Gregor Wurst. Washington, D.C.: National Geographic Society, 2006. [English Translation], ISBN 1-4262-0042-0
- *The Gospel of Judas* [3]. Eds. Rodolphe Kasser, Marvin Meyer, and Gregor Wurst. Washington, D.C.: National Geographic Society, 2006. [Coptic Transcription]
- Brankaer, Joanna, and Hans Gebhard-Bethge. *Codex Tchacos: Texte und Analysen*. Berlin: de Gruyter, 2007.
- Cockburn, Andrew. "The Judas Gospel." *National Geographic Magazine*. (May 2006): 78-95.
- DeConick, April D. *The Thirteenth Apostle: What the Gospel of Judas Really Says*. London: Continuum, 2007.
- Ehrman, Bart D. *The Lost Gospel of Judas Iscariot: A New Look at Betrayer and Betrayed*. Oxford: Oxford University Press, 2006.
- Evans, Craig A. *Fabricating Jesus: How Modern Scholars Distort the Gospels*. Downers Grove: Intervarsity Press, 2006. ISBN 0-8308-3318-8.
- Gagné, André. "A Critical Note on the Meaning of APOPHASIS in *Gospel of Judas* 33:1", *Laval théologique et philosophique* 63.2 (June 2007): 377-383.
- Gathercole, Simon J. "The Gospel of Judas." *Expository Times* 118.5 (February 2007): 209-215.
- Gathercole, Simon. *The Gospel of Judas: Rewriting Early Christianity*. Oxford University Press, 2007.
- Head Peter M. "The Gospel of Judas and the Qarara Codices: Some Preliminary Observations." *Tyndale Bulletin* 58 (2007): 1-23.
- Kasser, Rudolphe, Marvin Meyer, and Gregor Wurst. *The Gospel of Judas*. Commentary by Bart D. Ehrman. Washington D.C.: National Geographic, 2006.
- Kasser, Rudolphe, and Gregor Wurst. *The Gospel of Judas, Critical Edition: Together with the Letter of Peter to Philip, James, and a Book of Allogenes from Codex Tchacos*. Washington D.C.: National Geographic, 2007.

- Krosney, Herbert. *The Lost Gospel: The Quest for the Gospel of Judas Iscariot.* Washington D.C.: National Geographic, 2006.
- Meyer, Marvin, ed. *The Nag Hammadi Scriptures: The International Edition.* New York: HarperOne, 2007.
- Pagels, Elaine, Elaine Pagels and Karen L. King. *Reading Judas: The Gospel of Judas and the Shaping of Christianity.* New York: Viking, 2007. ISBN 978-0-670-03845-9
- Perrin, Nicholas. *The Judas Gospel.* Downers Grove: Intervarsity Press, 2006.
- Porter, Stanley E., and Gordon L. Heath. *The Lost Gospel of Judas: Separating Fact from Fiction.* Grand Rapids: Eerdmans, 2007.
- Robinson, James M. *The Secrets of Judas : The Story of the Misunderstood Disciple and His Lost Gospel.* San Francisco: Harper, 2006.
- Wright, N. T. *Judas and the Gospel of Jesus: Have we Missed the Truth about Christianity?* Grand Rapids: Baker Books, 2006.

- Gregory A. Page, *Diary of Judas Iscariot of the Gospel According to Judas* (1912, reprinted 1942, Kessinger Publishing)
- Lars Gyllensten, *Testament of Cain* (1963 Bonnier, Stockholm, Sweden; English translation in 1982, Persea)

External links

- The Gospel of Judas [4] PDF Version hosted by nationalgeographic.com
- L' *Evangile de Judas* sur Coptica.ch [5] - texte, index et traduction française
- The Lost Gospel [6] - online feature from National Geographic
- Early Christian Writings: [7] *Gospel of Judas*
- Patrick Baert, "Gospel of Judas back in spotlight after 20 centuries" [8]
- Judas stars as 'anti-hero' in gospel [9] - Julia Duin, *Washington Times* - April 7, 2006
- The Lost Gospel of Judas Iscariot? [10] - NPR
- Rodney J. Decker on the Gospel of Judas sensation (PDF, audio, and PowerPoint) [11]
- Michel van Rijn, "The Hunt for the Gospel of Judas" [12]
- Gospel of Judas does not deserve name 'gospel,' Jesuit scholar says [13]
- Text of Irenaeus, *Against Heresies*, regarding Gospel of Judas [14]
- Survey of Early Reaction to the Gospel of Judas - 100 citations [15]
- "The Betrayer's Gospel" -- Article from the *New York Review of Books* [16]
- The Betrayal of Judas - An overview of the translation controversy, from the Chronicle Review [17]
- Associations between the Gospel of Judas and the Coptic Orthodox Church [18] — the Coptic Orthodox Church's response to the alleged "Gospel" of Judas
- Not so secret gospels [19] – BBC article

Unknown Berlin Gospel

Unknown Berlin Gospel

The **Unknown Berlin Gospel** is a fragmentary Coptic text from an otherwise unknown gospel that has joined the New Testament apocrypha under the title ***Gospel of the Saviour***. It consists of a fragmentary fire-damaged parchment codex that was acquired by the Egyptian Museum of Berlin in 1961 (accessioned as Papyrus Berolinensis 22220). Its nature was only discovered in 1991, when it came round to being conserved (the sheer number of similar manuscripts being conserved causing the 30-year delay), and was revealed in a 1996 lecture by Charles W. Hedrick. It has been edited and translated into English by Hedrick and Paul Mirecki (Hedrick and Mirecki 1999) and by Bart D. Ehrman (Ehrman 2003). The fragmentary nature of the text admits of more than one sequential ordering of the contents, giving rise to more than one useful translation, and some public discussion (*vide* References).

The manuscript appears to date from the 6th century; Hellenisms in the vocabulary and grammar suggest that it was translated from a lost Greek original. The hypothetic original Greek text on which it is based is thought to have been composed somewhere in the late second or early third century, judging from the theology and style. The Gospel is not a narrative but a dialogue, a form often chosen in Antiquity for didactic material.

The content is heavily gnostic in that salvation is available only to those who understand the secret knowledge (*gnosis*), and also shows parallels with the Gospel of Peter, in that the significance of the Crucifixion is somewhat watered down, being considered a part of a heavenly journey, an idea much more in keeping with a gnostic world-view. The unnamed Saviour (assumed to be Jesus) engages in a dialogue with his apostles that is somewhat more personal than is found elsewhere. And at one point, the cross itself is addressed, as if it is a living creature, a companion rather than a device for death.

References

Chronologically:

- Charles W. Hedrick and Paul A. Mirecki, 1999. *Gospel of the Savior: A New Ancient Gospel* (Santa Rosa, California: Polebridge Press) ISBN 0-944344-68-2
- Stephen Emmel, 2002. "The Recently Published Gospel of the Savior (*unbekanntes Berliner Evangelium*): Righting the Order of Pages and Events," in *Harvard Theological Review* **95** pp 45-72 (abstract [1])

- Charles W. Hedrick, 2003. "Caveats to a 'Righted Order' of the Gospel of the Savior," in *Harvard Theological Review* **96** pp 229-238 (abstract [2]).
- Bart D. Ehrman, 2003. *Lost Scriptures: books that did not make it into the New Testament* (Oxford University Press). ISBN 0-19-514182-2

External links

- Early Christian Writings: The Gospel of the Saviour [3]
- Notes on the Gospel from an Interested Amateur [4]

Gospel of Mani

Gospel of Mani

For the 1956 "The Gospel of the Prophet Mani", see Duncan Greenlees.

The **Living Gospel** (also **Great Gospel**, **Gospel of the Living** and variants) is a lost 3rd century gnostic gospel written by Mani, originally written in Syriac and called the *Evangelion*, from the Greek: Ευαγγελιον ("Evangel") and one of the original scriptures of Manichaeism. A number of fragments are preserved in the *Cologne Mani-Codex* (discovered 1969) and on manuscript fragments found in Turfan beginning in 1904. Some Coptic manuscript fragments recovered at Fayyum appear to contain a sort of commentary or homily on the gospel.

It is known that the gospel had 22 parts, each labelled by a different letter of the Aramaic alphabet. The combination of two Turfan fragment allows the reconstruction of the text of the first part (*alaph*). The section deals with the nature of the "King of the World of Light" who resides at the "Navel of the World" but is also present on his whole earth, from without as from within, having no limits except where his earth borders on that of his enemy, the "Kingdom of Darkness". Schneemelcher (1990) suggests tentatively that the text may have been designed as a gospel of the gnostic type, perhaps intended to comment on or replace the Gospel of Jesus.

External Links

The Opening Words of the Living Gospel [1]

Gospel of Marcion

Gospel of Marcion

The **Gospel of Marcion** or the *Gospel of the Lord* was a text used by the mid-second century Christian teacher Marcion to the exclusion of the other gospels. Its reconstructed fragments now appear among the New Testament apocrypha. Many Catholic Christian apologists wrote treatises against Marcion after his death, in addition to the noted work of Tertullian, that it has been possible to reconstruct almost the whole of Marcion's *Gospel of the Lord* from their quotations. Marcion, then, is known only through his critics, who considered his doctrines a deviation from orthodox Christianity.

Relationship to the Gospel of Luke

There are two possible relationships between Marcion's gospel and the Gospel of Luke.

Marcion as revisionist of Luke

Church Fathers wrote and the majority of modern scholars agree that Marcion edited Luke to fit his own theology, Marcionism. The Early Church writer Tertullian noted,"expunged [from the Gospel of Luke] all the things that oppose his view... but retained those things that accord with his opinion" This view is consistent with the way he altered other books in his canon such as the Pauline texts. It is also likely because Luke's gospel was believed to be complete by Marcion's time.

In it, he eliminated the first two chapters concerning the nativity and beginning at Capernaum and made modifications of the remainder suitable to Marcionism. The differences in the texts below highlight the Marcionite view that, first, Jesus did not follow the Prophets and, second, the earth is evil.

Luke	Marcion
O foolish and hard of heart to believe in all that the prophets have spoken (24:25)	O foolish and hard of heart to believe in all that I have told you
They began to accuse him, saying, 'We found this man perverting our nation . . .' (23:2)	They began to accuse him, saying, 'We found this man perverting our nation . . . and destroying the law and the prophets.'
I thank Thee, Father, Lord of heaven and earth... (10:21)	I thank Thee, Heavenly Father...

Gospel of Marcion   62

Marcion as pre-dating Luke

Some authors such as Charles B. Waite in 1881 *History of the Christian Religion to the Year Two-Hundred* suggested that Marcion's Gospel may have preceded Luke's Gospel. John Knox (not the same as the Scottish reformer John Knox) in *Marcion and the New Testament* also defends this hypothesis. For an example of evidence that may support this view, compare Luke 5:39 to Luke 5:36-38. In the 2006 book *Marcion and Luke-Acts: a defining struggle*, Joseph B Tyson makes a case for not only Luke but also Acts being responses to Marcion rather than Marcion's gospel being a rewrite of Luke.

Justification

Theologian Adolf von Harnack - in agreement with the traditional account of Marcion as revisionist - discusses the reasons for his alterations to Luke. According to von Harnack, Marcion believed there could be only one true gospel, all others being fabrications by pro-Jewish elements, determined to sustain worship of Yahweh. Furthermore, he believed that the true gospel was given directly to Paul by Christ himself, but was later corrupted by those same elements, who also corrupted the Pauline epistles. He saw the attribution of this gospel to "Luke" as another fabrication. Marcion thus began what he saw as a restoration of the original gospel as given to Paul.

Von Harnack writes that:

> *For this task he did not appeal to a divine revelation, any special instruction, nor to a pneumatic assistance [...] From this it immediately follows that for his purifications of the text - and this is usually overlooked - he neither could claim nor did claim absolute certainty.*

See also

- Papyrus 69 - possibly it is a witness of the Marcionite edition of Luke's Gospel
- Marcion

External links

- Marcion: The Gospel of the Lord [1]: five of the original total twenty-one chapters (in English)
- G.R.S. Mead, *Fragments of a Faith Forgotten* (London and Benares, 1900; 3rd edition 1931) [2]: pp. 241–249 Introduction to Marcion
- The Marcionite Research Library [3]: contains a full text in English
- History of the Christian Religion to the Year Two-Hundred by Charles B. Waite [4]: It includes a chapter where he compares Marcion and Luke
- *Marcion and Luke-Acts: A Defining Struggle* by Joseph B. Tyson [5] A case in favor of the view that the canonical Luke-Acts duo is a response to Marcion. Tyson also recounts the history of scholarly studies on Marcion up to 2006.

Gospel of Truth

Gospel of Truth

Gnosticism
This article is part of a series on Gnosticism
Early Gnosticism
Syrian-Egyptic Gnosticism
Gnosticism in modern times
Philo
Simon Magus
Cerinthus
Valentinus
Basilides
Gnostic Gospels
Nag Hammadi library
Codex Tchacos
Askew Codex
Bruce Codex
Gnosticism and the New Testament
Gnosis
Neoplatonism and Gnosticism
Mandaeism

Manichaeism
Bosnian Church
Esoteric Christianity
Jnana
Gnosticism Portal

The **Gospel of Truth** is one of the Gnostic texts from the New Testament apocrypha found in the Nag Hammadi codices ("NHC"). It exists in two Coptic translations, a Subachmimic rendition surviving almost in full in the first codex (the "Jung Codex") and a Sahidic in fragments in the twelfth.

History

The Gospel of Truth was probably written in Greek between 140 and 180 by Valentinian Gnostics (or, as some posit, by Valentinus himself). It was known to Irenaeus of Lyons, who objected to its Gnostic content and declared it heresy. Irenaeus declares it one of the works of the disciples of "Valentinius", and the similarity of the work to others thought to be by Valentinus and his followers has made many scholars agree with Irenaeus on this point.

> But the followers of Valentinus, putting away all fear, bring forward their own compositions and boast that they have more Gospels than really exist. Indeed their audacity has gone so far that they entitle their recent composition the Gospel of Truth, though it agrees in nothing with the Gospels of the apostles, and so no Gospel of theirs is free from blasphemy. For if what they produce is the Gospel of Truth, and is different from those the apostles handed down to us, those who care to can learn how it can be show from the Scriptures themselves that [then] what is handed down from the apostles is not the Gospel of Truth.

After its Coptic translations and their burial at Nag Hammadi, the text had been lost until the Nag Hammadi discovery.

Style

The text is written with strong poetic skill (notable even in translation), and includes a heavily cyclical presentation of themes. It is not a "gospel" in the sense of an account of the works of Jesus of Nazareth, but is better understood as a homily. The text is generally considered by scholars one of the best written texts in the whole Nag Hammadi collection, considering its worth highly as both a great literary work and a gnostic exegesis on several gospels, canonical and otherwise.

The work cites "Galatians, John, 1 John, Revelations, Matthew, 1 Corinthians, 2 Corinthians, Ephesians, Colossians, and Hebrews" from the New Testament. Of these it cites the Johannine Gospel the most often. It is also influenced by Thomas, for instance at one point (22.13-19) it cites John 3:8 alongside Thomas 28.

Content

The text describes a theory of the rise of Error in personified (female) form. The ignorance and yearning to see the Father bred fear, which coalesced into a fog by which Error gained power.

It then describes Jesus as having been sent down by God to remove the ignorance. Jesus was a teacher confounding the other scribes and teachers, and asserted they were foolish since they tried to understand the world by analysing the law. But Error grew angry at this, and nailed Jesus to a tree. It also proceeds to describe how it is knowledge that grants salvation, which constitutes eternal rest, describing ignorance as a nightmare.

Having next described the parable of the good shepherd, in an esoteric manner, it then describes how feeding the hungry and giving rest to the weary is to be understood as feeding spiritual hunger, and resting the world weary.

This is followed by a parable about anointing, the meaning of which is obscure, but may be connected with the way in which a sealed amphora meant it was full, a metaphor for knowledge - having the final "seal" in the jigsaw and you understand, but without it, the scraps of understanding you have put together can still be easily undone:

> But those whom he has anointed are the ones who have become perfect. For full jars are the ones that are usually anointed. But when the anointing of one jar is dissolved, it is emptied, and the reason for there being a deficiency is the thing through which its ointment goes. For at that time a breath draws it, one by the power of the one with it. But from him who has no deficiency no seal is removed, nor is anything emptied. But what he lacks the Perfect Father fills again.

Aside from a final description of achieving rest by gnosis, the remainder of the text concerns a treatise on the connection between the relationship between the Son and the Father, and the relationship of a name to its owner. The prime example of this is the phrase it uses that *the name of the Father is the Son*, which is to be understood in the esoteric manner that the *Son* is the *name*, rather than as meaning that *Son* was a name for the *Father*.

Relation to Valentinian Fragments

Layton printed eight fragments of Valentinian literature, each a quote a Church Father claimed to take from the Valentinian corpus although none from the "Gospel of Truth". Layton further noted where the excerpts agree with one another.

"Fragment G", which Clement of Alexandria (Stromateis 6.52.3-4) related to "On Friends", asserts that there is shared matter between Gnostic Christian material, and material found in "publicly available books"; which is the result of "the law that is written in the [human] heart". Layton relates this to GTr 19.34 - when Jesus taught, "in their hearts appeared the living book of the living, which is written in the Father's thought and intellect". Both rely on a shared concept of pre-existent yet obscured knowledge, which emanated from the Father of the Gnostics.

"Fragment F" also comes from the Stromateis, 4.89.1-3. Directed to the Gnostics, it calls the congregation "children of eternal life" and hopes that they will "nullify the world without being yourselves nullified". Layton relates the former to GTr 43.22 at the end of the work, which emphasises that the Gnostics are the Father's children and will live eternally. Layton relates the latter to GTr 24.20, which proposes to "nullify the realm of appearance" and then explains this as the world that lacks the Father.

The concept that fear and the lack of knowledge are connected is evident;

> *Having entered into the empty territory of fears, he (Jesus) passed before those who were stripped by forgetfulness, being both knowledge and perfection, proclaiming the things that are in the heart of the Father, so that he became the wisdom of those who have received instruction.*

There is also the mentioning of an awakening brought about through the acquiring of knowledge, and the dismissal of that which is not real, namely fear. Fear is not real because it does not come from the Father. That which is not light is not from the Father, such as a tree only brings forth one fruit, the Father's only fruit is light.

The level to which these writings express the power of the "self" in the coming of knowledge, and the conflict of the innate perception that the average person is too weak, too full of misconceptions to be able to lift themselves up is addressed. A theme in the Gospel is the idea that we each have the mechanism within us to change, to awake, rather than the Father having to implant us with these gifts in order for a change to occur.

References

- Bentley Layton, "The Gnostic Scriptures", The Anchor Bible Reference Library, Doubleday, NY 1987.
- Harold W. Attridge and George W. MacRae, "The Gospel of Truth (Introduction and Translation)", from *The Nag Hammadi Library*, James M. Robinson (ed.), pp. 38-51
- Text of the Gospel of Truth [1]

Gnostic Gospels

Gnostic Gospels

Gnosticism
This article is part of a series on Gnosticism
Early Gnosticism
Syrian-Egyptic Gnosticism
Gnosticism in modern times
Philo
Simon Magus
Cerinthus
Valentinus
Basilides
Gnostic Gospels
Nag Hammadi library
Codex Tchacos
Askew Codex
Bruce Codex
Gnosticism and the New Testament
Gnosis
Neoplatonism and Gnosticism
Mandaeism

Manichaeism
Bosnian Church
Esoteric Christianity
Jnana
Gnosticism Portal

The **Gnostic Gospels** are gnostic collections of writings about the teachings of Jesus, written from the 2nd - 4th century AD. These gospels are not part of the standard Biblical canon of any major Christian denomination, and as such are part of what is called the New Testament apocrypha. Recent novels and films that refer to the gospels have spurred public interest.

History

The word *gnostic* comes from the Greek word gnosis, meaning "knowledge", which is often used in Greek philosophy in a manner more consistent with the English "enlightenment". Some scholars continue to maintain traditional dating for the emergence of Gnostic philosophy and religious movements. It is now generally believed that the evidence suggests that Gnosticism was a Jewish movement which subsequently reacted to Christianity or that Gnosticism emerged directly in reaction to Christianity. The name "Christian gnostics" came to represent a segment of the Early Christian community that believed that salvation lay not in merely worshipping Christ, but in psychic or pneumatic souls learning to free themselves from the material world via the revelation. According to this tradition, the answers to spiritual questions are to be found within not without. Furthermore, the gnostic path does not require the intermediation of a church for salvation. Some scholars, such as Edward Conze and Elaine Pagels, have suggested that gnosticism blends teachings like those attributed to Jesus Christ with teachings found in Eastern traditions.

Dating

See also Gnosticism

The documents which comprise the collection of gnostic gospels were not discovered at a single time, but rather as a series of finds. The Nag Hammadi Library was discovered accidentally by two farmers in December 1945 and was named for the area in Egypt where it had been hidden for centuries. Other documents included in what are now known as the gnostic gospels were found at different times and locations, such as the Gospel of Mary, which was recovered in 1896 as part of the Akhmim Codex and published in 1955. Some documents were duplicated in different finds, and others, such as with the Gospel of Mary Magdalene, only one copy is currently known to exist.

1. The Gospel of Thomas is held by most to be the earliest of the "gnostic" gospels composed. Scholars generally date the text to the early-mid second century. The Gospel of Thomas, it is often claimed, has some gnostic elements but lacks the full gnostic cosmology. However, even the description of these elements as "gnostic" is based mainly upon the presupposition that the text as a whole is a "gnostic" gospel, and this idea itself is based upon little other than the fact that it was found along with gnostic texts at Nag Hammadi. Some scholars including Nicholas Perrin argue that *Thomas* is dependent on the *Diatessaron*, which was composed shortly after 172 by Tatian in Syria. A minority view contends for an early date of perhaps 50, citing a relationship to the hypothetical Q document among other reasons.

2. The Gospel of the Lord, a non-gnostic but otherwise non-canonical heretical text, can be dated approximately during the time of Marcion in the early 2nd century. The traditional view holds Marcion did not compose the gospel directly but, "expunged [from the Gospel of Luke] all the things that oppose his view... but retained those things that accord with his opinion" The traditional view and dating has continued to be affirmed by the mainstream of biblical scholars, however, G. R. S. Mead have argued that Marcion's gospel predates the canonical Luke and was in use in Pauline churches.

3. The *Gospel of Truth* and the teachings of the Pistis Sophia can be approximately dated to the early 2nd century as they were part of the original Valentinian school, though the gospel itself is third century.

4. Some gnostic gospels (for example Trimorphic Protennoia) make use of fully developed Neoplatonism and thus need to be dated after Plotinus in the 3rd century.

Selected gospels

Though there are many documents that could be included among the gnostic gospels, the term most commonly refers to the following:

- Gospel of Mary (recovered in 1896)
- Gospel of Thomas (versions found in Oxyrhynchus, Egypt in 1898, and again in the Nag Hammadi Library)
- Gospel of Truth (Nag Hammadi Library)
- Gospel of Philip (Nag Hammadi Library)
- Gospel of Judas (recovered via the antiquities black market in 1983, and then reconstructed in 2006)

References in popular culture

The gnostic gospels received widespread attention after they were referred to in the 2003 best-selling novel *The Da Vinci Code*, which uses them as part of its backstory. The novel's use of artistic license in describing the gospels stirred up considerable debate over the accuracy of its depiction. As a result of public interest triggered by the novel and film, numerous books and video documentaries about the gospels themselves were produced which resulted in the gnostic gospels becoming well-known in popular culture.

The 1999 film *Stigmata* uses the discovery of an as-yet unknown gnostic gospel as the basis for the story. The end of the film also makes references to the Catholic Church's denunciations of such texts as being heretical.

The 2008 novel, *Change of Heart*, by Jodi Picoult, also makes several in-depth references to the gnostic gospels - and to the Gospel of Thomas in particular.

See also

- *The Missing Gospels: Unearthing the Truth Behind Alternative Christianities*
- Historical Jesus
- Docetism
- Jesus Seminar

Gospel of Basilides

Gospel of Basilides

The **Gospel of Basilides** is a "lost" text from the New Testament apocrypha by Basilides, mentioned by Origen, Jerome, Ambrose, Philip of Side, and the Venerable Bede. It was composed in Egypt around 120 to 140 A.D. In all likelihood, this gospel was compiled of canonical gospels, the text being shortened and altered to suit Basilides's Gnostic tenets, a diatessaron. or harmony, on Gnostic (*Docetic*) lines.

Papyrus Oxyrhynchus L 3525

Papyrus Oxyrhynchus L 3525

Papyrus Oxyrhynchus L 3525 is a copy of the apocryphal Gospel of Mary in Greek. It is a papyrus manuscript formed in a roll. The manuscript palaeographically had been assigned to the 3rd century. It is one of the three manuscripts and one of the two Greek manuscripts of the Gospel of Mary. It is shorter than Papyrus Rylands 463.

Description

Survived only small fragment of a single sheet (probably roll). The fragment is broken on all sides. The fragment covers the material contained in 9.1-10.10 of the Coptic manuscript. The reconstruction of the missing parts (especially the starts and ends of the lines) is not an easy task and depends on the Coptic text. There are some differences between Greek fragment and the Coptic text.

It was written in ca. 50 letters per line. The nomina sacra are written in abbreviated form. The manuscript was discovered in Oxyrhynchus. The text was edited by P. J. Parsons. The manuscript currently is housed at the Papyrology Rooms of the Sackler Library at Oxford with the shelf number P. Oxy. L 3525.

See also

- Gospel of Mary
- Oxyrhynchus Papyri
- Papyrus Rylands 463

Further reading

- P. J. Parsons, *3525: Gospel of Mary*, in *The Oxyrhynchus Papyri* (London: Egypt Exploration Society, 1983).
- D. Lührmann, *Die griechischen Fragmente des Mariaevangeliums POxy 3525 und PRyl 463*, Novun Testamentum 30 (1988), 321-338.

External links

- Image: P.Oxy. L 3525 [1] (© Copyright [2] the Egypt Exploration Society).
- P.Oxy.LXXII 3525 [1] from Papyrology at Oxford's "POxy: Oxyrhynchus Online"
- P. Oxy. 50.3525 [2] - exact transcript
- Christopher Tuckett, *The Gospel of Mary*, Oxford 2007. [3]

Papyrus Rylands 463

Papyrus Rylands 463

Papyrus Rylands 463 is a copy of the apocryphal Gospel of Mary in Greek. It is a papyrus manuscript in roll form. The manuscript has been assigned palaeographically to the 3rd century. It is one of the three manuscripts and one of the two Greek manuscripts of the Gospel of Mary. It is longer than Papyrus Oxyrhynchus L 3525 (POxy 3525).

Description

Only a small fragment of a single sheet (probably roll) has survived. The fragment is broken on all sides and contains the material contained in 7.4-19.5 of the Coptic manuscript. The reconstruction of the missing parts (especially the starts and ends of the lines) is not an easy task and depends on the Coptic text. The Greek text can only be conjectured on the basis of the Coptic version. The manuscript is fragmentary but shows two errors.

There are some differences between the Greek fragment and the Coptic text. The nomina sacra are written in abbreviated form. The text was edited by C. H. Roberts in 1938. The manuscript currently is housed at the John Rylands Library (Gr. P. 463) at Manchester.

See also

* Gospel of Mary
* Papyrus Oxyrhynchus L 3525 - another Greek manuscript of the Gospel of Mary

Further reading

* Roberts, C. H. (1938) *Gospel of Mary* in: *Catalogue of the Greek and Latin Papyri in the John Rylands Library, Manchester.*
* Lührmann, D. (1988) *Die griechischen Fragmente des Mariaevangeliums POxy 3525 und PRyl 463*, in: *Novum Testamentum*; 30 (1988), pp. 321-338.

External links

- P. Ryl. 463 [2] - exact transcript
- Christopher Tuckett, *The Gospel of Mary*, Oxford 2007. [1]

The Secret Gospel of Mark and the Synoptic Problem

The Secret Gospel of Mark and the Synoptic Problem

The Secret Gospel of Mark and the Synoptic Problem examines how the Secret Gospel of Mark, discovered by Morton Smith, relates to the Synoptic Gospels. Helmut Koester hypothesized this relationship, specifically in reference to the formation of "Canonical" Mark. This article will analyse Koester's theory, as well as its criticism by Scott G. Brown. Secret Mark's relation to the Gospel of John is also examined, as well as the question of the text's authenticity.

Koester's Theory

Helmut Koester has done considerable work in the past on the Synoptic problem. To begin with, his theory presupposed the Two-source hypothesis, and was concerned with the issue that the text found in the canonical version of Mark could not have been the same as the one used by Matthew and Luke. Koester took a cue from recent studies of the Gospel of John at the time he was writing and believed that the Gospel of Mark was written in several stages . Koester concluded that the original version of Mark that was written around 70 CE is now lost, but set out to reconstruct the stages which eventually lead to the production of "Canonical" Mark. Koester's reconstruction was different in that it included the Secret Gospel of Mark as part of the process that lead to canonical Mark. It is as follows:

Stage 1a: The first stage in Koester's theory begins with what he deems Proto Mark, believing it to be the form of Mark's Gospel that was used by the author of Luke's gospel. Koester believed that Proto Mark was probably the oldest form of Mark, though he thought it likely that it was proceeded by several written sources that had at least been partly translated from Aramaic, which he believed had many of the Markan miracle stories and the Passion Narrative.

Stage 1b: This was what Koester believed to be an expanded variant of Proto Mark, which incorporated new miracles into Mk 6:45-8:26. Koester believed that the author of Matthew's Gospel used this variant. Koester also thought that it was not impossible that this variant proceeded the copy used by Luke, in which case Luke would have used a defective copy of Proto Mark.

Stage 2: In this stage of redaction, Koester saw Matthew's Gospel as a thorough revision of Proto Mark. Koester believed that Matthew added five major speeches of Jesus, with materials drawn from

Mark and especially from Q as a major structural element. Miracle stories were also assembled in Matt. 8-9.

Stage 3: In which Luke revised Proto Mark in a different way.: he followed the outline of Proto Mark in the first and third sections of his Gospel, but in the second section, what is commonly called the "travel narrative", added materials drawn from Q and a special Lukan source.

Stage 4a: Whereas Matthew and Luke modified Proto Mark in order to create new Gospels, Proto Mark's own development, which Koester believed resulted in "Canonical" Mark, preserved a more intact version of the original outline of the Gospel. The style and language was also maintained, and as a result Koester assigned this development to the Markan community. However, Koester believed that Secret Mark could be seen as a stage of revision in between Proto Mark and "Canonical" Mark.

Stage 4b: In which a different edition of Secret Mark was used by the Gnostic sect known as the Carpocratians. Clement of Alexandria, in his letter to Theodore that was discovered by Morton Smith, alleged that the Carpocratians added to Secret Mark various "pollutions", such as nocturnal homosexual teachings.

Stage 5a: Koester felt that a number of features which distinguish Proto Mark from Canonical Mark have ties to the Secret Gospel. This belief of Koester's lead him to conclude that "Canonical" Mark is derived from Secret Mark. The difference between the two, according to Koester, is that the redactor of "Canonical" Mark omitted the story of the raising of the youth in Secret Mark, and yet another incident in Mk. 10:46. Koester felt that the redaction of Proto Mark which produced Secret Mark must have occurred in early second century CE. According to Koester's reconstruction, "Canonical" Mark would have been written sometime thereafter, but before Clement wrote his letter to Theodore. Koester believed that the Carpocratians based their edition of Mark on an unabbreviated version of Secret Mark. Although Clement believed that "Canonical" Mark was written before Secret Mark, Koester believed that the truth was in fact the reverse, that "Canonical" Mark was a "purified", abbreviated version of Secret Mark since he also believed that traces of Secret Mark were still visible in "Canonical" Mark.

Stage 5b: Koester believed that the addition of Mk.16:9-20 to the end of "Canonical" Mark showed that history of "Canonical Mark" was still continuing. Although there are Markan features in the longer ending, Koester felt that the further history of the Markan text was most deeply influenced by the two major revisions of Proto Mark by Matthew and Luke .

Scott G. Brown's Criticism of Koester's Theory

Scott G. Brown has criticized Koester's Theory, arguing that "Canonical" Mark is not an abbreviated version of Secret Mark, but rather that Secret Mark is an expanded version of Canonical Mark. Brown argues that Secret Mark probably contained more than the fifteen sentences quoted by Clement of Alexandria. Clement, in his letter to Theodore, describing the Secret Gospel as "mystic", says that Mark transferred those things from his notes that were "suitable towards the study of knowledge". Brown argues that the Alexandrian Church used "Canonical" Mark for instructing catechumens and Secret Mark for expounding more "secret knowledge", that is, *gnosis*, the unwritten secrets of the Alexandrian Church. Furthermore, Brown argues that there must have been enough material in Secret Mark for it to be used for advanced, theological instruction. He argues further that Clement's letter indicates that Secret Mark was very different - and much longer - than the "Canonical" Mark, and that it didn't omit anything from the Canonical version .

According to Brown, Secret Mark was not the product of a small redaction, whereby the redactor of the Secret Gospel subsequently eliminated only the two pericopae mentioned by Clement in his letter and thus created the "Canonical" version. What is being dealt with is something on a much larger scale.

Under Koester's theory, Brown argues, the redactor would also have taken away the other mystical traditions found in the Secret Gospel, and would have reverted the text back to something much closer to proto-Mark. But, in such a case, according to Brown, why would then the redactor also overlook Mk. 14:51-52, and the smaller changes that spawned the minor agreements in Matthew's and Luke's Gospels against Mark's? Why and how, then, would the redactor do this? Brown argues that, if the situation described above is what actually happened, the reason for it would remain elusive.

It would have to be explained why the more spiritual elements would have been taken out of "Canonical" Mark - and the Gospel therefore "despiritualized" - especially at Alexandria, where the exegesis of spiritual dimensions was undertook by many. Brown concluded that the idea of a Markan Priority based on Secret Mark didn't add up, and that Koester's theory was simply too problematic .

Instead, Brown believes that it made more sense for the shorter, "Canonical" Gospel to be expanded into the longer, spiritual Gospel of Secret Mark by the Alexandrians. Brown noted that the total disappearance of Secret Mark and proto-Mark under Koester's theory is also harder to account for. How is it, Brown asked, that the version of Mark used by Matthew and Luke in 80s CE leaves us no trace, but somehow Secret Mark is able to influence all the other copies that come after it, including "Canonical" Mark? Once again, Brown thought that the situation proposed by Koester did not make much sense. The triumph of "Canonical" Mark over a widely dispersed proto-Mark, Brown argues, would have required some sort of official policy of replacement, but yet there is no proof whatsoever for such a policy ever taking place . Brown thus concluded that it made more sense to believe that the Alexandrians expanded "Canonical" Mark into the longer, Secret Gospel for the purpose of higher, spiritual teaching that was not circulated outside of the Alexandrian Church .

Secret Mark's Relationship to the Gospel of John

Although it is not directly related to the Synoptic Problem, Secret Mark also shares a relationship with the Gospel of John. Morton Smith noted that the pericope of the resurrection of the young man by Jesus in Secret Mark bore similarities to the story of the raising of Lazarus in John's Gospel. Smith felt that the author of John did not know about Secret Mark, and that the story of Lazarus's resurrection in John's Gospel was an independent expansion of the pericope of the raising of the youth, that is also found in Secret Mark . F.F. Bruce, however, has argued that the pericope of the raising of the young man is too clumsily based on the Lazarus pericope found in John, and that the pericope found in Secret Mark is not an independent Markan counterpart to the Lazarus pericope .

Criticism Concerning the Authenticity of Secret Mark

In 1958 Morton Smith was cataloguing the contents of the library of the monastery of Mar Saba, when he claimed to have came upon copy of Isaac Voss's edition of *Six Letters of Ignatius*, which was published in 1646. He claimed to have found a copy of a letter by Clement of Alexandria in the back of the book to a person named Theodore, in which Clement quoted from Secret Mark and Smith's discovery has been accepted by a large number of scholars as being authentic. Some authors however, such as Stephen Carlson in his book *The Gospel Hoax: Morton Smith's Invention of Secret Mark*, have accused Smith of fabricating a hoax. If Secret Mark is a hoax, then the issue of it being connected to the Synoptic Problem is made null and void. Therefore, it shall have to be examined here, albeit briefly. In the November/December 2009 issue of *Biblical Archaeology Review*, Hershel Shanks wrote an article summarizing rather concisely the debate surrounding the authenticity of Secret Mark. It will be referred to here for its summarization of the arguments against Secret Mark's authenticity.

There are two major arguments in favor of Secret Mark being a hoax:

1. Morton Smith had the scholarly expertise required to create the hoax.

2. The document (referring here to Clement's letter to Theodore) contains flaws and anachronisms that affirmatively show that it is a hoax .

If Smith did hoax Secret Mark he would have to be capable in the following areas, according to Shanks:

> "1. He would need to know enough to forge the two fragments of Secret Mark. Thus, he would have to be an expert in composing Greek, but also in New Testament textual criticism sufficient to fool a text critic like Harvard's Helmut Koester.
>
> 2. Smith as forger would also have to be an expert in Clement, the purported author of the letter, as well as in the various subjects, like the Carpocratians, mentioned in the letter. He would also have to have sufficient knowledge of Latin to forge the Latin passage in the letter.
>
> 3. Finally, he would have to be an expert in 18th-century handwriting (paleography), when the second-century Clement letter was apparently copied in the back of the copy of a 1646 edition

(by Isaac Voss) of the letters of Ignatius of Antioch ."

Even if the document is a hoax, Shanks notes that it does not prove that Smith is the hoaxer. Shanks also points to three flaws in Clement's letter that have been alleged to demonstrate that Secret mark is a hoax. Firstly, there is a reference to salt being adulterated with another substance in the letter that is an anachronism: that technology that is being referenced is a modern one. The only way salt can be adulterated is if it is poured. In order for it to be poured, it would first have to be granulated, a technology that the people in Clement's time did not have access to. Stephen Carlson also thinks that this is a reference to the Morton Salt Company, a clever pun on Smith's own name and a hint towards the identity of the hoaxer. The second flaw has to do with how homosexuality is portrayed in the letter. Shanks notes that Pearson has asserted that the view of homosexuality found in Clement's letter is to be rooted in the middle of the twentieth century, one that would be inconsistent with how homosexuality was viewed in ancient Greco-Roman culture. The third flaw also features another anachronism: Clement is referred to by the title *Stromates*. This is seen as anachronistic, Shanks says, because the letter was apparently written in the late second or early third century and Clement was not known by the title of *Stromates* until later . Finally, Stephen Carlson has noted a fourth flaw in Clement's letter. Carlson has observed the shakiness of the handwriting in the letter, a phenomenon known as *forger's tremor*, as well as the retouching of letters, the inclusion of twentieth century letter forms and the letter too closely imitating Clement's writing style until the end. Carlson alleges that all of these things point to the fact that Secret Mark is in fact a hoax . Despite pointing out numerous things that have been used to condemn Secret Mark as a hoax, Shanks remains objective in his overall view of the controversy, concluding that in the end the controversy simply pits one scholar against the other .

See also

- Gospel of Mark
- Markan priority

Article Sources and Contributors

Gospel of Thomas *Source*: http://en.wikipedia.org/?oldid=388779475 *Contributors*: 1 anonymous edits

Nag Hammadi library *Source*: http://en.wikipedia.org/?oldid=387381337 *Contributors*: Hardyplants

Secret Gospel of Mark *Source*: http://en.wikipedia.org/?oldid=381064557 *Contributors*:

Gospel of Philip *Source*: http://en.wikipedia.org/?oldid=389089464 *Contributors*: 1 anonymous edits

Gospel of Mary *Source*: http://en.wikipedia.org/?oldid=385984312 *Contributors*:

Gospel of Judas *Source*: http://en.wikipedia.org/?oldid=387344142 *Contributors*: Varlaam

Unknown Berlin Gospel *Source*: http://en.wikipedia.org/?oldid=367805925 *Contributors*:

Gospel of Mani *Source*: http://en.wikipedia.org/?oldid=378768522 *Contributors*: Jimhoward72

Gospel of Marcion *Source*: http://en.wikipedia.org/?oldid=390626465 *Contributors*: Editor2020

Gospel of Truth *Source*: http://en.wikipedia.org/?oldid=379390615 *Contributors*:

Gnostic Gospels *Source*: http://en.wikipedia.org/?oldid=388718113 *Contributors*:

Gospel of Basilides *Source*: http://en.wikipedia.org/?oldid=369600435 *Contributors*:

Papyrus Oxyrhynchus L 3525 *Source*: http://en.wikipedia.org/?oldid=386183183 *Contributors*:

Papyrus Rylands 463 *Source*: http://en.wikipedia.org/?oldid=385986549 *Contributors*:

The Secret Gospel of Mark and the Synoptic Problem *Source*: http://en.wikipedia.org/?oldid=372620623 *Contributors*: Dyuku

Image Sources, Licenses and Contributors

CPSIA information can be obtained at www.ICGtesting.com
Printed in the USA
LVOW09s1425230216

476361LV00009B/86/P